Chasing a Dream…

Chasing a Dream…

✦

When reality does not live up to the fantasy.

A Memoir

Alice Jo Marlin

iUniverse, Inc.
New York   Bloomington

Chasing a Dream
When reality does not live up to the fantasy.

iUniverse books may be ordered through booksellers or by contacting:

iUniverse
1663 Liberty Drive
Bloomington, IN 47403
www.iuniverse.com
1-800-Authors (1-800-288-4677)

Because of the dynamic nature of the Internet, any Web addresses or links contained in this book may have changed since publication and may no longer be valid. The views expressed in this work are solely those of the author and do not necessarily reflect the views of the publisher, and the publisher hereby disclaims any responsibility for them.

ISBN: 978-1-4502-1439-1 (sc)
ISBN: 978-1-4502-1440-7 (ebook)

Printed in the United States of America

iUniverse rev. date: 03/29/2010

*My heartfelt thanks to my daughter Dianne
who edited this book,
scanned, retouched and captioned the photos
and also designed the cover.
This book would not have been possible
without her generous contributions.*

Dedicated to my three children:
Jesse, Dianne and Mariane.

I look inside my closet
Amazed at what I see
Fragments of my life
Scattered in front of me

Pictures of my children
As they grew day by day
Boxes full of cobwebs
Gathered along the way

Books and bits of paper
Filled with stories still unwritten
Many papers missing
In the depth of consciousness, hidden

Hangers from the ceiling
Suspended gracefully, empty now
Waiting for the grand finale
To fill them up somehow

So many loose ends remaining
That I can hardly find
The time to straighten out and tidy
The closet of my mind

Alice Jo Marlin

Prelude

I saw the knife in his hand and I froze. For what seemed like an eternal moment, I was rooted to the floor. In one hand he held the knife while the other was clenched in a fist. I felt sure that I was going to die… but he turned and stabbed the door behind him making three deep gashes. Three hard hits in a frantic rage, arm high above his head, then he slid to the floor in a heap. A shiver rushed through me. My legs seemed to take on a life of their own. I grabbed my youngest daughter, who had just entered the room, and we ran outside to a neighbor's house. This was the turning point… there was no going back. A war of nerves had begun. An end to a love affair that had started at the close of WWII. It had been a promising beginning for a young girl with a big dream…

Contents

Chapter One

My Early Years in Malta

With my wide eyes peeled on the darkening afternoon sky, my father and I stood next to a bomb shelter watching a familiar sight. We had just witnessed another air battle between British Spitfires and German Messerschmitts and seen the German Stukas drop their bombs on our devastated island. Two Stuka war planes had been hit and, as we watched, enemy parachutists floated down to earth.

It was the beginning of 1941; I was nine years old. Air attacks by German and Italian planes were a daily occurrence and at great cost to our small island of Malta. Located in the middle of the Mediterranean Sea, Malta was a stronghold fortress for the British and American forces in the European battleground of WWII. With Italy to the North and Africa to the South, we were surrounded by enemy waters.

The island is a solid rock, but everything on it had been reduced to rubble. Our deep Catholic religious faith and headstrong patriotism towards the British and their allies were our salvation during these momentous times.

A siren screamed its high pitched 'RAID IS PAST' signal, but we could still see the parachutists coming down and we could hear security vans speeding towards the area. I followed the path of one of the parachutes as it drifted and rose higher with each gust of wind. Grabbing my father's hand, I asked,

"Daddy, why is that parachute not landing?"

My father, who was gazing at it through his binoculars, took a long time to answer, as if the words were unable to leave his throat. Finally, mainly talking to himself and without looking at me, he said,

"The pilot has been shot. Half his body has been severed off. There might not be enough weight and it could take some time before he will come down." Then as an afterthought he added, "I am sure he is dead and not feeling any pain."

I was not old enough to grasp the full meaning of that statement, although I have never forgotten it.

It was not always like this. I remember a time before the war started, when my mom and dad used to have friends over for a joyful evening visit. After a few drinks and some canapés they would all gather in the parlor where my mother played the piano and she and my father sang operatic duets. The guests would join in a lively chorus.

Both my mother and father loved opera. My father had a strong baritone voice so when he sang an aria and my mum played an operatic stanza, neighbors would actually stop by and jokingly ask,

"Mary, is that Caruso on the radio?" And my mother would teasingly reply,

"No, but John thinks he is!"

La Traviata and *Rigoletto* could be heard often in our house and almost made the walls shake with the reverberation of music and song. While my brothers, sister and I were usually sent upstairs to bed, the beautiful sound of my mother's piano playing and all the singing voices on these special days filled me with happiness. Sleeping was not on my mind. Many times I would climb out of bed and sit halfway down the spiral staircase, trying to get a peek at the gathering below without being noticed.

One of the things that stand out in my memory about my parents is how different their personalities were. Before they were married my mother had studied languages and could speak fluent Maltese, English, Italian and French. She also enjoyed a competitive game of tennis. She had attended private schools and came from a family of fifteen children although eight of them had died in childhood. She grew up with five older brothers and one younger sister. Large families were common at the start of the 20th century. In spite of her education, my mother was very timid. Her five older brothers were very protective towards her but also very strict and domineering, which I believe resulted in her having low self esteem.

On the other hand my father had traveled extensively throughout Europe, was self assured and had a jolly disposition. He had four living siblings, two brothers and two sisters of whom he was the youngest. The men of his family were in the medical profession. His brothers were pharmacists and his father was a doctor. He started out as a medical inspector with the Public Health Department and worked up to become Superintendent and Health Adviser for the island. He had the responsibility for the health of the island's people regarding communicable deceases, inoculations, isolations and preventative measures during epidemics, which were common at the time. When a child came down with a contagious disease, such as measles, whooping cough, diphtheria or mumps, it became necessary to quarantine the home. A sticker would then be placed on the door warning visitors of the infection and thus hopefully avoid an epidemic. This was specifically intended for pregnant women and mothers with young children who might have visited.

My father was also very rigid in giving us kids cod liver oil, which we hated. It was slimy and thick and smelled awful. I gagged every time I had to swallow a spoonful. Mum would give us candy afterwards to freshen our breath. Another preventative measure of my dad's was coating our throat with a brush dipped in iodine. We accepted all this as a requirement for our own good. Eventually the Red Cross brought us some needed vaccines.

Commonalities of my parents were their love of family, their Catholic faith and their passion for the opera. A big difference between them was in how they disciplined my siblings and me. Basically, my mother did not know how. She preferred to say,

"Wait until your father gets home and I tell him what you did."

This did not go well with me as the suspense lasted all day until father came home from work, and when he learned about our skirmishes, he would spank us. I resented my mother's attitude and threat more than my dad's actual spanking, even though he often used a belt. Maybe it's because after the spanking he would explain why he had to do it and most of the time my father was affectionate. He was also the one who would tuck us in bed at night and tell us stories. Sad to say, I do not recall my mother kissing or hugging me and. although she never raised her hand on me, I remember her as cold and incapable of showing affection. She never made use of her many talents after she got married. Her primary function was aimed at tending to my father's needs and cooking for the family. These were activities that she loved doing and at which she excelled. We had a nanny-housekeeper to help with the household chores and take care of us kids while mother was busy cooking. Yet the more prominent my father's profession became, the more mother seemed to lose her self-confidence. There was no question that my father ruled the family. I suspect that's how it was in those days.

Our house was made of stone slabs cut from a quarry. With the climate of the island being sub-tropical, hot and humid, we sweltered in the summer. We used fans, but they only managed to swirl the hot humid air around us. We had indoor plumbing, electricity and running water but no air conditioning or forced-air heat. In the hot summers my brothers and I used to slip off our beds at night and sleep on the floor's cool ceramic tiles. On cold winter nights my parents used to light a freestanding kerosene heater. We placed it in the center of the room and mother would put a kettle on top of it so the steam added humidity to the dry air. We would all gather around the heater until the room warmed up and then we would snuggle under our cold bed sheets while father filled hot water bottles to place at the foot of our beds. If any of us had a hint of a cold, mother also added Vicks to the kettle's water so it then became a vaporizer.

People's health had to be of primary concern to my father. I remember him coming home from unsanitary areas he had overseen and putting his hands up in the air as soon as he entered the front door. This was a signal for us not to touch him. He would then go directly to the bathroom, remove all his clothes, shower and then douse his clothes in the bathtub filled with disinfectant. When he ran out of disinfectant, petrol (gasoline) was substituted. My mother would later rinse them and air them out on a drying clothes line in the sun for days, to dispel the smell of the petrol. In wartime we had no dry cleaners.

Water had to be heated on the stove for bathing, clothes washing and dish cleaning. These kitchen stoves were not gas or electric but fueled with petrol, something like our modern day camp stoves. A funnel that was lowered or raised by turning a front knob controlled the flame. The petrol was delivered by a man pulling a horse-drawn wagon and sold in refillable bottles.

Hot freshly baked bread was also delivered by wagon, but the baker rode in front and guided the horse to several stops along the street. He did not have to stop at every house. A crusty hot slice of fresh bread covered with melting butter was the best tasting thing in the world to me, a craving I have to this day. I also remember the tin-smithing man coming down the street pulling a horse. This horse pulled a cart that had pots and pans hanging on each side of it. They would clang together as he held the reins and walked slowly down the street. The noise from the banging pots and pans alerted the whole neighborhood of his arrival and anyone who had a cooking utensil that was rusting or leaking and needed to be sanded and resoldered came out to their front door for his services.

Every weekday in the early morning, farmers came down the street with vegetables and fruit loaded on carts pulled by donkeys. Each farmer would yell his wares,

"Tomatoes, come and get your tomatoes!" or "Who wants potatoes, onions, carrots and lettuce while they are nice and fresh?"

The milk arrived via a goat herder and his flock. Each customer had their own container and he proceeded to milk the goat right there in the street at their front door. We had no lawns in front of our houses, only narrow sidewalks. The lead goat, guided by a rope and wearing a collar of bells, heralded the coming of the milkman.

After the vegetables and the fruit were bought and sold, the milk and bread delivered, and the streets were again cleared, we kids claimed them as our play area. We played Bocci, we played games with marbles and beads, we skipped rope, and when it rained we sailed paper boats down the gutter into water drains. Girls had their dolls and boys had their toy soldiers. We flew kites. As we grew up, boys relished playing soccer and girls favored table tennis. When I was very young, I even made my own paper dolls. Figures of girls were cut out from sales catalogues that my mother brought home, and then I glued them to a cardboard backing. I also cut out cardboard to make three-dimensional doll furniture and drew on the details. Mirrors were made from tinfoil found in my uncle's discarded cigarette packages.

We had no washing machines; however, we did have a washerwoman who came once a week. She cleaned all the bed linen, towels, underclothes, sleepwear, and other washables. In the absence of a water heater, she placed a large galvanized tub on a stand over a small stove. As the water in the tub heated, she shaved soap from a large square bar and added it to the hot water. She used a wooden dowel to stir the soap foam as the clothes were put in. This went on for about half an hour after which she would scrub the clothes on a washboard. Later the clothes would be lifted out and placed in another tub filled with cool clear rinsing water and then hung on an outside line to dry in the sun. These weekly washes took up most of the day.

Most houses in Malta, as in other European cities, were and still are like what we would call townhouses. The structures are tall and narrow with access to the flat roofs. They have a common wall between them and, more often than not, had no insulation so anyone having an argument or a loud conversation could easily be heard through the walls. Lucky for us, since my parents loved to sing opera so often, they tended to drown out neighborhood noises. Also, my father was a radio buff, and so music and songs were frequently heard throughout our house. I started piano lessons from my Aunt Evelyn when I was only seven years old. She was a popular piano teacher and lived only two short blocks from us. Unfortunately, the war started soon after and the lessons ended.

In the late evening when we kids were tucked in bed and the summer heat was too much for the adults to stay indoors, one of our neighbors would rig up a light above the outside of his front window. Tables and chairs were then brought out and many of the neighborhood adults played cards for pennies while others just relaxed, chatted or embroidered and thus enjoyed companionship in the cooler evening air. These were the coveted summer night social hours for my parents; as for us kids, the summer days were our highlights.

One big day that we all looked forward to every summer was when our whole neighborhood street of about ten houses chartered a bus. The big event was an afternoon and evening picnic outing by the sea. Mothers spent all morning fixing picnic lunches while we counted the minutes until the bus was scheduled to arrive. We got very excited as the bus seemed huge and filled the width of our narrow street. The day was always picked for its full moon and we would all eagerly board the bus to one of our beautiful sandy beaches. The trip took about 45 minutes and soon after we arrived we unfolded the blankets and food hampers and all enjoyed a wonderful picnic. While the parents cleared things away we kids built sandcastles, picked sea shells, chased each other playfully and, finally, happily settled to watch the sun go down and the full moon rise in all its glory.

It was then that we deliriously headed towards the shimmering and still warm waters and it was delightful. We would splash to our heart's content and stay at the beach until after midnight. When we boarded the bus to head back home, the adults broke into song and we kids curled up in blankets and rested our sleepy heads on any lap we could find, returning back to our street, our home and our beds, engulfed in the memories we had gleefully made.

My father had a greyhound dog named Muzette that he loved very much. He acquired her before marrying my mother. I remember the old dog got pitifully sick and became very timid and afraid. If there was a thunderstorm, she would hide under the bed and whine. When I was about six years old, she tried to take a piece of bread from my hand and slightly bit me. This upset my mother so much that eventually dad had to put his dog to sleep. I remember him crying over this. I do not think that my mother ever liked Muzette. Dad used to tell the story that before he and mum got married he had told her that she had to accept him with the dog or neither of them.

We also had cats that both parents loved. They were allowed to sleep in bed with us, and my father used to hold his favorite cat around his neck like a collar. I used to dress up the kittens in dolls' clothes and push them around in a doll carriage. They never made a fuss and would just lie there and go to sleep. One unusually smart cat used to play hide-and-seek with me. She stayed downstairs until I went upstairs, hid, and then called her. She would then come and look for me and when she finally found me, she would run and beat me down the stairs. After, she'd meow until I went and hid again.

We had a young maid named Carmen who was in her late teens. Her duties included helping mum with the house cleaning and, in the afternoons, taking my brothers and me to the nearby seaside. My two younger brothers were pushed in a stroller while I walked along side. This gave my mother free time to go shopping and to cook dinner.

On the maid's day off, my mother would take us to the seashore herself. On these days my father always came to meet us on his way home from work. He rode a motorcycle in the summer, and in his white safari-type outfit and English Bombay hat he made a splendid figure. I could hardly wait for his arrival. I used to feel so proud watching him because to me he was not just my dad in a white suit and Bombay hat on a motorcycle but my knight in shining armor riding a gallant horse.

My father was a very handsome man. He had dark wavy hair and deep brown eyes, and a dimple marked the center of his chin. Despite his authoritarian ways he was also very jovial, playing with us and carrying us around. Whenever we had a cold or started to cough, he would be the one at night who rubbed us down with a medicated ointment, placed a heated flannel cloth on our chest and recited stories to us until we fell asleep.

When my mother was still single she had dressed in beautiful clothes, played tennis and taken piano lessons. She had short brown curly hair and grayish blue eyes. She was slim and tall and held herself proud. After she got married and had children she gave all her energy to being a housewife and mother and neglected other outlets and interests. She must have been disappointed, yet because this was the way things were expected of her, she managed to keep her frustration deep inside. Maybe she was not even aware how it affected her, but it was evident in her frequent complaining and in her gaining weight. Dad established the rules of the house and when they went out for the evening she had to pass his inspection. I actually remember him telling her to take off some of her lipstick or to pin her dress neckline up higher.

Santa Claus did not come when I was young. Christmas was strictly a religious occasion, although our parents did give us a few presents twelve days later, on January 6th during the feast of the Epiphany. On that day, the three kings had followed the star and arrived at the stable to give Baby Jesus their gifts. Our uncles, aunts and grandparents used to give us money to buy something for ourselves. Alas, mother usually kept the money and took us to the store to buy things we needed, like clothes and shoes, not toys or games. One time I received a gift from my Aunt Yolly that started my lifelong unquenchable desire to read. It was the hardcover book called *Hiawatha* by Robert Louis Stevenson. I vividly remember the beautiful colored pictures and how I read and reread that book for many years after. From then on, reading has always given me great pleasure.

We had no Christmas trees either, as they were not the focus of the Holy Season and did not even grow on the tropical island. What we always had was a Baby Jesus made of wax, about nine inches long, lying in a manger on a straw bed. Two weeks before Christmas we planted wheat seeds in small tin containers and placed them around the manger. By Christmas Day, the wheat would have sprouted and looked like beautiful grass. We then surrounded this with lit candles and thus we celebrated the day that Christ was born. Some relatives and friends displayed larger nativity scenes, a few being very elaborate and stretching more than six feet across. These included shepherds with their flock, the three kings, stone houses, camels and donkeys, and even people on cobbled streets. Ever since, I have always longed for such a beautiful display. My parents usually attended mass early in the morning and then mother spent the day cooking the turkey dinner and baking pastries. The turkey was not roasted but cooked on top of the stove in a large pot with vegetables, which became a huge amount of turkey soup that was usually served before the main meal.

I loved to read and study and received high marks in school. I also enjoyed sketching and my schoolmates always asked me to draw pictures for them which I loved doing. But in my day and culture, girls were only supposed to grow up to become housewives and mothers. At that time, intelligence was considered wasted on a girl. For me to go to work would be a disgrace, as only women who suffered economic needs were expected to work. A career was never discussed or suggested for a woman.

My brother Ronnie, three years younger than me, had always been the studious type. He received good grades in school too, especially in math. Since my parents encouraged him, at times I felt they favored him. Besides being very obedient, he was always ready to tell on me if I did anything that I was not supposed to do. Quiet and serious in his demeanor, he grew up to be a reputable accountant.

On the other hand, brother Joe, six years younger than me, did not particularly like school. He would rather be with his friends playing soccer. On a couple of occasions he failed to pass his final exams, and my parents had to provide him with private lessons during the summer so that he could rejoin his classmates and be admitted to the next grade. In my teen years I became closer to my brother Joe in spite of the difference in years because he was easier to please and more receptively compliant. He grew up to be a newspaper photographer, then a reporter and eventually had his own column specializing in immigration, at the *Toronto Star* newspaper in Canada.

As for my younger sister Marlene, there were eight and a half years between us. When WWII started I was eight years old and she had just been born. When I got married at 19, she had only turned 11; so sad to say, we did not have the opportunity to share many experiences in our childhood, though I do remember resenting that I had to take her with me everywhere I went. At first it was as a big sister looking after her baby sister and later she was my chaperon the few times I went out with friends. As an adult, Marlene worked in a convalescent home caring for elderly patients. She is compassionate and gives of herself freely as a volunteer in many church and school organizations.

I know that I can depend on all three of my siblings in time of need.

Chapter Two

The Devastations of WWII

I was eight years old when Italy's Premier Mussolini joined Hitler in declaring war against the allies in 1939. My family lived in Sliema, one of the two main cities encircling the main harbor of Malta. The other was Valetta, the capital of the island.

These cities and our two airports, Luqa and Ta' Qali, were the most vulnerable to an attack, and curfew was quickly established on the island.

The British Colonial government in Malta instructed everyone to put heavy drapes or blankets across windows and to turn off lights by sunset each night. My father, who was well known in the community, was quickly enlisted by the local police to patrol the streets and to make sure no lights shone through the windows and that everyone was off the streets and in their home by nightfall. He wore a helmet and had permission to carry a gun. On his arm he wore a band with the letters A.R.P. identifying him as a member of an Air Raid Precaution unit. I was so proud of him, and I felt sure he would protect us and keep us from harm.

Our island is very close to Italy, just below the 'boot,' only about 60 miles south of Sicily. Although Malta was at the time a British Protectorate, we also had very close cultural ties with Italy. We vacationed there, and our main religion was Roman Catholic like theirs. We studied both English and Italian languages in our schools. Maltese cuisine included many British traditions, like afternoon tea and scones, fish and chips and mutton stew; however, we also enjoyed meals of Italian spaghetti and lasagna. Wine with dinner was also standard. Additionally, Maltese culture had adopted Italian opera, fine arts and song festivals. Many Maltese women were married to English or Italian men. It became very hard to differentiate our emotions and to accept that the Italians were now our enemy.

Soon after war had been declared we began to experience life in underground bomb shelters. These shelters were hewn from the limestone rock foundation, first dynamited and then finished with pickaxes. The Italians raided us from the very onset of the war, coming in at high altitude to drop their bombs. They certainly intimidated us, causing fear, anger and personal losses. By the end of 1941, when the Germans joined in the bombing attacks on the island, our situation worsened. The Germans swooped down low and pounded us with bombs constantly. According to war statistics, there were 2,931 air raids over Malta in 1942. The attackers were determined to erase the island from the map and blow us out of the sea. They had also tried and failed to invade the island with U-Boats. There is hardly a family in Malta that did not lose one or more of its loved ones during the war.

As the war escalated, many people lost their homes. My Uncle Josie was a successful wine maker and owned a large house in the country village of Rabat. He was ordered by the government to open his home and take in people who now had nowhere to go. Rather than invite strangers, he offered shelter to all his relatives, especially those like us who lived in vital target areas. As we moved, my family had to leave behind all our possessions because we would all be now living together in just one large room. I was only allowed to take one toy and I chose my favorite teddy bear. While I initially resisted the move, when I met my other cousins, I soon appreciated having so many playmates. Still, with all the rooms in the house full, we were very crowded. We were about eight families in all sharing the house and about thirty of us were children ranging in age from one year to eighteen. Uncle Josie was instructed to paint stars near his front door, each one representing a family being housed within. This showed that he was fulfilling his obligation to house the needy.

Uncle Josie, who was married to my father's sister Edwidge, was a very unique person with many interests. He played the piano, composed music and also studied languages. He imported soil from Italy for his orchids, roses and tropical gardens, as well as grapes and sugar from

Sicily for the winery that produced the 'Pulverenti' wine label, a favorite on the island. He had close ties with Italy and at the start of the war his whole family started studying the German language… in case the war took a different turn.

This house was actually quite a big mansion, spread out on a hill above my uncle's manufacturing plant. These facilities included three large warehouses with huge vats of fermenting grapes and machinery for wine bottling and labeling. The house's beautiful library, den and living room were now used as bedrooms to accommodate all the families but not the music studio, which was his private sanctuary. The gorgeous gardens were sacrificed to accommodate pigs, goats and chickens. We kids eventually even transformed the large water fountains and lily ponds into swimming pools. In retrospect, I realize how devastating this intrusion and war episode must have been for his family. I was only 11 years old at the time and too young to comprehend the tremendous sacrifices they made on our behalf. It turned out to be our salvation because, as suspected, our house in Sliema suffered a direct bomb hit.

My uncle hired workers to dynamite under the beautiful gardens to construct a large bomb shelter with compartments for each family. For most of 1942 we lived underground as German bombers from Sicily did not give us any reprieve. We felt safe in this shelter and endured the dampness with beads of salt and water trickling down the sides of the walls.

Eventually we learned to decipher the drone of the planes and knew if they were incoming or outgoing. We were even able to distinguish if they were enemy or friendly aircraft. At times we cautiously ventured out of the shelters; parents to wash or cook and children to engage in much needed play. One of our games was to rush outside after an air raid and look for hot shrapnel. We would measure them against each other's, and the one who found the biggest piece was the winner. There were no toys to buy so we made our own. We created a checkerboard with cardboard and painted colored squares. We used stones to move across the board and fashioned a die from glued cardboard squares. We even made the game *Battleship* from cardboard and held the colored paper ships in place with straight pins. We were proud of our ingenuity. For exercise we skipped rope. Boys played soldiers and hunted an imaginary enemy, while girls played at being nurses, imitating the military presence on the island.

New clothing and shoes were both scarce and expensive. I remember my father stuffing cardboard in the soles of our shoes to cover the holes. At times, dad managed to make us new insoles cut out from pieces of discarded rubber tires. He also made tin cups out of used milk cans. He sawed the can in half, bent down the rough edges, formed a handle from the top part of the can and then soldered it to the side.

Soon my parents had no food to offer us as there was nothing to buy. Sugar, bread and powdered milk were sparsely rationed. The government introduced the 'Victory Kitchens' where we lined up for hours to be doled soup or goat stew, a bowlful for each member of the family. My mother smartly divided the rationed sugar, powdered milk and bread and gave my brothers and me our own portions. This way, rather than crying for more, we knew that we had received our allotment and used it sparingly, guarding it closely and priding ourselves that we still had some left when the next ration portion came due, in about one or two weeks depending on government supplies. Our baby sister was only two years old at this time so mother took care of her share.

One day, as the sirens wailed, we could distinctly hear enemy airplanes approaching. The sounds grew closer and louder. My mother yelled for us to return to the shelter. I was playing checkers with my cousin Hina, Uncle Josie and Aunt Edwidge's daughter, 18 months older than me. I could hear my mother calling again and finally ran towards the shelter stairs while Hina stayed behind picking up the game pieces to bring down to the shelter. Seconds later, I felt the impact of a huge explosion and was thrown flying, down the stair's shaft and onto the shelter floor. On this day, the Messerschmitt fighter planes with Spitfires in pursuit had been staging a dogfight and because of their ongoing gunfire we had not heard the Luftwaffe Stuka dive bombers approaching. The bomb blew out all the front rooms of the big house.

My father had been upstairs watching the air fights from an open window and my mother panicked with fear, concerned for his safety. I remember her screaming and calling his name. She did not know exactly where he was and did not want to leave us. Though unhurt, I felt lost in the thunderous roar of walls collapsing and dust rushing down to engulf me. The falling dirt from the explosion also obscured the entrance to the shelter and the blast blew out our oil lamps and plunged us into darkness. Eventually someone lit up candles and we finally glimpsed my father through the dust as he entered the shelter. As the debris settled and the candlelight reached him, we could see that he was covered with caked-on blood and dirt. Fresh blood was also dripping from his head and both his arms where numerous tiny shrapnel had hit him as he raised his arms to protect his face. In the darkened shelter, to me, he looked like the crucified Jesus. I trembled with fright for a moment, but then we all ran up to him and hugged him and held him and thanked God he was alive.

But where was Hina? What had happened to her?

I kept thinking, *She had not been far behind me, so why hadn't she come to the shelter?* We heard hurried steps coming down the stairs and my uncle and aunt appeared. My aunt was hurt. She had white dust all over her body and was clutching one side of her head with both hands. My uncle explained to us that the two huge mirrors that were on each side of the grand stairway had fallen and shattered, and she had been hit by a mirror splinter. Between sobs she kept asking

"Has anyone seen Hina, is she here?"

I knew she was not in the shelter, since I had not seen her coming down the stairs and I remembered that she was still picking up our game when I had been blown down the shelter by the blast. My fears mounted as I wondered, *Where could she be?*

We then became aware of heavy boots stomping in the rooms above us, and we heard British soldiers searching for anyone who might be wounded. One soldier came down the shelter to let us know that a couple of workers from my uncle's winery had been seriously injured and needed to be taken to the hospital immediately. One of them had lost a leg and the other had a stomach wound. An army truck had been provided for their transport. My father, still bleeding from both arms, decided to accompany them to the hospital.

When the siren sounded the 'all clear,' I made an attempt to leave the shelter hoping to find my cousin Hina. The soldiers held me back and informed us all that it was dangerous to go upstairs because the whole house might be very unstable, as they did not yet know the extent of the damage. We could do nothing except sit and pray. Somebody started to recite the rosary as we always did in times of peril. It seemed to calm us down.

Then what we feared most happened. A soldier came down the shelter again and speaking in a low voice to my uncle and aunt informed them that Hina had been found. She had been killed, blown apart by the bomb. Some of her body parts had been found scattered in the front of the house. My aunt screamed and then fainted. My uncle sobbed as he ran up the stairs and this time the soldiers did not hold him back.

I was stunned. We had been playing together just an hour before. She was not only my cousin but also my best friend. I was now 12 years old and she was 14. Together, we had begun to notice boys, mostly friends of my cousins. She had taught me how to put on lipstick and press my lips to a napkin to leave an imprint and then show it to the boys who would try to snatch the napkins from our hands. Now she was gone. I did not even cry. I was in shock and could not make myself believe that this really happened. Later I learned that the soldiers had placed what they found of her on an army cot and had searched all night for her other missing body parts. My uncle and aunt were devastated. How ironic that they had both done so much to protect our families and it was their own daughter to be the one to die. The sight of our protective home in rubble, the wailing sound of the bomb as it neared our house, the vibration of the blast as it hit, the loss of my dear cousin, my father's injuries and the horror of it all remain vivid in my mind.

My uncle's house was on a hill overlooking Ta' Qali airport. Two other large houses positioned in a triangle on top of the hill had been occupied by the British armed forces and used as barracks. A treed area surrounded the properties and we children used to hang ropes from the branches of a large oak tree and tie on old rubbers discarded from car wheels to use as swings to play on. At other times we would tie a long piece of plywood on to the strongest branches on each end and four or five of us cousins would sit in the middle of it while another would stand on each end and push the swing sideways. It was a lot of fun. But as the war escalated, an anti-aircraft gun had occupied this area. Many times I had witnessed the earth below explode in the distance as I watched German planes dive, hit their target and turn back, followed by an anti-aircraft barrage from the ground. The Stuka bombers were black against the daylight sky and were very hard to see at night. Their deadly sound was telltale though, and we knew where they were before they were caught in the crossbeams of the numerous searchlights.

Looking back I now realize that the reason I did not feel more devastated when my dear cousin and best friend died was because I did not have time to mourn.

In less than an hour we again heard the wailing siren informing us that another air raid had hit the small island. It did not take long for the German planes to reach us from Sicily, only 60 miles away. Sometimes enemy planes left Sicily while the earlier bombers were still above the island; so the 'raid is past' siren never had the chance to be activated and the raids lasted all day and night. Ground-to-air barrage never stopped and the danger of bombs falling on our heads remained a constant possibility. Daily casualties on Malta were high and this time it had been us. This day I lost my cousin and came close to losing my father. We had almost become immune to the slaughter or maybe we had psychologically accepted it so we could continue to function.

With enemy planes above our heads day in and day out, our primary focus became the ability to show strength and courage in the face of coming to grips with death. My other cousins and I continued to hang together and tried to make the most of each day and probably did not know enough to worry about the next day as our parents surely must have done.

Going to school was a challenge. There were no busses or private cars in operation as petrol had to be saved for the armed forces. Even my father, who had been accustomed to going to work in a chauffeur driven car, had been resigned to riding his bicycle. More often than not, while walking to school the air raid warning siren would sound and I would scurry to find shelter or hide in doorways. If my schoolmates and I heard no sound of planes close by, we would continue to our school at St Joseph's Convent in Rabat.

Once there the nuns then took us down to a large common shelter shared with others in the village. Being a school with about 200 children from first grade to sixth, we were allowed a certain area to accommodate us. There was an iron gate at each end of our space and long benches were carved out of the rock on each side of a narrow aisle and we squeezed together as best we could with some of us sitting on the damp floor in between. Beyond the gate we could see the local people, some of them farmers. Even the sheep, goats and pigs would be down in the shelter if they happened to be out in the few small pastures nearby when the raid alarm sounded. Mostly though, the animals would have been cooped up in pens as the shelters were meant specifically for people. However, we enjoyed the pigs' squeals and the sheep's bleats, as they were a diversion from the sounds of war going on above our heads.

Although my uncle's house had suffered the majority of damage from the bomb, the apparent target had been the anti-aircraft gun, which had been hidden under the trees at the top of the hill where the three big houses stood. It had been placed there to protect the Ta' Qali airport that could be plainly seen from my uncle's house. After the bombing, the house was declared safe to live in except for the front rooms and the garage that had been demolished and cordoned off limits. For weeks after the tragedy my uncle closed himself up in his music studio with his piano, composing music and poems in memory of his daughter Hina.

Hina's sisters, who were in their late teens, used to date some of the English pilots stationed at Ta' Qali. Upon returning from chasing the enemy out to sea, these pilots would swoop low over our house before landing at the airport to let my cousins know that they were safely back. We kids would run up to the roof and wave at them to our hearts' delight.

Hina's brother Aldo, who is a year younger than me, became my best friend. Maybe each of us substituted for his sister and we became almost inseparable. We swam in the former fishponds in the garden and we rode the trucks carrying the wine bottles from the cellars beneath the house to a storage warehouse in the port village of Marsa. My uncle, being a businessman, had a permit for petrol to run his trucks. I even played with Aldo's toy soldiers and planned strategies for attack against the soldiers of the other cousins.

In the spring, the rebuilt garage was turned into a kite-making assembly. About ten cousins would get together, cut and glue kites and avidly try to beat each other's creativity by making the longest tail, mixing the brightest colors or extending the widest rib span. It is amazing how we managed to find the ways and means to occupy ourselves. The kites were made of colored tissue paper and the ribs were cut out of bent bamboo and, of course, flour and water was the glue that held the kites together. It was love, laughter and the ability to rebound that kept us children able to overcome the daily onslaught of war.

Soon however, things got even worse. Vegetables and fruit became scarce as they began to be sold on the black market while butter and cheese were mostly unobtainable.

My father managed to get some canned cheese from the N.A.A.F.I. (Navy, Army, Air-Force Institutes) canteen through a friend in the Air Force. This was the United Kingdom's official trading organization geared to provide supplies to the British military at home and abroad. During the war it was hard to reach the island so supplies were few and far between. When he opened the can we found it to be covered in green mold. He started slicing around and around until he reached the yellow central part that appeared to be edible. To us it was like finding the pearl in the oyster!

A great percentage of the Allied ships trying to reach Malta were sunk before they entered our Grand Harbour. The ships had to pass through the Strait of Gibraltar to enter the Mediterranean Sea and then pass by Spain and North Africa. Malta was trapped between Sicily and Tunis. The island was close to the end of its resources and a date had even been predicted for its surrender. It was unthinkable that Malta would be allowed to die.

My father told me that preparations had been made, under the order of Winston Churchill, for an immense armada to come to the aid of Malta. 'Operation Pedestal' was its code name and it was to take priority over all other demands of the Royal Navy. Fourteen cargo ships carrying food and arms were launched and escorted by 59 naval warships. The convoy was heavily attacked and only five of the cargo ships reached our harbor. The American Texaco-owned tanker 'OHIO' was one of them. She carried thousands of tons of much needed gasoline. A direct hit had blown up her boiler and her pumps died. With tons of water in her sagging hull but still holding her cargo, she was strapped between two destroyers and towed in. Crowds of people lined up on the Maltese bastions to watch and welcome her and their cheering never stopped as she limped into the harbor.

Then the war took a strategic turn. The British and the American Forces had been able to push back Rommel's army from Tangier and Alamein. The German armies were also now divided between the European front and the Russian advance. Malta now became the base for backing the British in Africa and also the American and the British commanders in their planned invasion of Italy. Malta became an essential supply link. Air raids over Malta subsided as the Germans now had their hands full at other fronts. The island had survived.

To this day I vividly recall the hunger, the ration coupons, the Victory Kitchens the devastation of the buildings all around us, the sound of bombs whizzing by, and the dreaded explosions. The daily fears of not knowing who had survived and who did not, or if any of our friends or relatives had been hit. I remember singing odes to Churchill and praying to God. Daily gatherings around the radio for news and standing at attention in silence during the rendition of *God Save the King* when the news ended became a ritual. This psychology helped us to keep our courage up under very drastic conditions. Yet in spite of it all, while adults must have been living under constant stress and deprivation, we children somehow managed to find moments of daring, excitement and make-believe. Even girls played with toy soldiers and toy guns while our older sisters and cousins took pleasure in making dresses out of salvaged silk parachutes. The mighty Germans could not destroy our island of Malta, neither our spirits.

In December of 1943, President. D. Roosevelt visited Malta and presented the island with an illuminated scroll in a lovely wooden case, on behalf of the American people.

It said in part:

"Under repeated fire from the skies, Malta stood alone and unafraid in the center of the sea, one tiny bright flame in the darkness – a beacon of hope for the clearer days which have come."

The citation presented for "valorous service far above and beyond the call of duty" was later reproduced in bronze and placed in Valletta's main square as a permanent monument.

Chapter Three

End of the War

During my childhood years from eight to twelve, World War ll raged on and my childhood play activities imitated those wartime experiences. I remember how I played with rubber band powered planes and used marbles as bombs. Since I had more boy cousins than girl cousins, I often played the more masculine games. We enjoyed table games like dominoes, chess and monopoly and when we got tired of those we improvised by building towers with playing cards.

Although we enjoyed the large fishponds that had been turned into swimming holes, many hours were also spent playing in the bomb shelter. Imbedded in the rock we would find pockets of soft lava that we used as putty, forming animal shapes and farm buildings. Shrapnel from the exploded bombs were our coveted trophies. Our parents must have been overwrought with worry about us and surely were glad to see how we managed to play and take pleasure in whatever was available.

In the spring, we flew our kites and creatively crafted parachutes for them. We tied the four corners of handkerchiefs with a stone in between, and then we threaded the kite string through an empty spool of thread and hooked the kerchief to the spool with a paper clip. As the March wind blew and the kite soared up to the sky, the spool, the string and the toy parachute went up with it. A good tug would release the clip and the weight of the stone brought the kerchief gently back down to earth. As we got better at this, we became more creative, at times tying a toy soldier at the end. It was quite ingenious.

In 1943, my father and I began to prepare our home in Sliema for our family's return. Workmen had repaired the structural damage and now my dad started fixing and painting the doors and windows while I dusted and washed. I was barely thirteen and would make the journey from Rabat to Sliema riding behind my father on his motorcycle.

It was on one of these occasions that we met an old friend of dad's and stopped to chat. In an amiable manner his friend said,

"Why John! Is that lovely lady, in the seat behind you, your daughter or your girlfriend? She looks so grown up."

I blushed, nevertheless I felt very flattered. The compliment made me beam with gratitude and I was glad to be with my dad. To my great disappointment he replied,

"Yes, she is my daughter and we're on our way to our house to get some work done, but she is not much help."

I was crushed. For the rest of the day I cleaned and dusted and cried, feeling that no matter how much I tried, it was not going to be good enough for my father. Even today, instead of the compliment, I recall more vividly the insult. I am sure that my father did not realize how much his random remark hurt me. I deeply believe that the wounds created with words can have just as permanent an effect as physical trauma.

When you are young and eager to please, a comment like that can affect your self-esteem for many years to come. Weeks later, when cleaning again, instead of trying to do my best I merely made a mediocre effort. *After all,* I told myself, *I was not appreciated. If my best was not good enough, why try so hard?*

An old English proverb says,

"Sticks and stones may break my bones, but words will never hurt me."

Believe me…it is not true.

Soon we were able to finally leave my uncle's house and his family's great hospitality and move back to our own home. By 1945 the war was nearly over and when V-E Day came the whole island celebrated. Fireworks lit up the skies and ships in the harbor shot ballast from their cannons. Churches tolled their bells and the streets were filled with people hugging, singing and rejoicing.

To celebrate, my parents went to my grandmother's house where her children still lived. Grandma Helen was my mother's mother and had lived around the corner from us. Here they were met by my other uncles and aunts. Soon toasts were being drunk and bottles of Whiskey and Gin kept being replenished. Since my parents were very strict and hardly ever let me out of their sight, it was a big surprise that they allowed me to go with a school friend down to the seafront to watch the fireworks, which was about a mile away. I became enthralled with joy and enthusiasm and the mood was exhilarating. Service men were tossing their caps in the air and everyone was kissing everyone else. An American sailor threw me his cap and I felt like a princess wearing it like a crown.

The jubilation continued but after a few hours, as the sky turned darker and the celebrations became more boisterous, I felt that I should be returning home. Letting me come to the wharf with my friend on this special day had been an exceptional permission from my parents and I did not want to abuse it. My friend agreed and we both started up the street towards home.

The streets were very crowded so we did not notice that two sailors were following us. Laughter filled the air and everyone seemed very excited. We reached my friend's house and as we bid each other goodbye, one of the sailors stopped to talk to her while the other followed me. Soon he caught up with me and placed an arm around my shoulders. This was the first time in my life that a man had put his arm around me other than my father. I impulsively pushed him away, but he laughed and came even closer. I could smell liquor on his breath and he seemed a little unsteady, but his twinkling eyes seemed to dance as he smiled at me and it made me feel happy. He did not talk much other than happily shouting, "The war is over!" every now and then. I felt a kinship towards him. After all, this was V-E day and he was one of the service men stationed on my island that had protected us all.

Pretty soon we reached the side street leading to my grandmother's house where my parents were. At the corner of the street was a public bomb shelter that was now dark and empty. My grandmother's house was only a short distance up the street, but as we turned the corner and passed by the entrance to the shelter the sailor pushed me against the inside wall and started kissing me. He put both his arms around me and pulled me to him. His hands then traveled to my breasts and I became petrified. Conflicting thoughts raced through in my mind. He was older and stronger than me yet somehow I was not afraid of him. While I wanted to innocently hug him I soon realized this was not what he had in mind. I had had no experience with men pressing against me and with his increasing excitement I wanted to get away. An idea came to my rescue.

"Wait, wait," I whispered close to his ear, "my parents are expecting me home any minute and they will soon come looking for me. Let me go and tell them that I have returned and that I'm with my girlfriend and I will come right back. Then I can stay with you longer."

Believing me, his hands dropped to his side. I ran to grandmother's house, pushed the door open and slammed it shut behind me. I had no intention of going back out again. I could feel my face flushed and my heart was beating so fast and hard that I had to stop in the hallway to catch my breath. Loud voices and music were coming from the dining room. I entered the room and nobody noticed me. None of my relatives were aware that I had experienced my first flush of sexual excitement. Nobody knew that a young man had fondled and kissed me and stirred new emotions within me, emotions of desire and also emotions of fear and panic. I thought about my sailor the rest of the night, but I was glad to be safely home with my own little secret.

Grandma Helen had passed away in July of 1939 just before the war started. Her house had been the family gathering place before the war and even now after. My uncles, Paul and Infantino (Fantin), and my Aunt Evelyn were all still single and lived there and we continued to refer to it as 'Grandma's house.'

I remember going there when I was just six or seven years old, before we had moved. At Easter time I used to help Grandma make large cookies in the shape of boys and girls. They would be about six inches long and one of each figure was placed on the other with a filling of marzipan in between. After they were baked, we decorated them with colored icing and placed a chocolate egg in their center. We used raisins for eyes and M&Ms for buttons and called them 'Figolli.'

During family visits, Grandma would make us intricate paper dolls and read us stories while she sat in a big armchair with all her grandchildren at her feet surrounding her. When we resumed our get-togethers at war's end, I really missed her.

Aunt Evelyn, who had been teaching me piano lessons before the war, now started to teach me how to cut and sew my own dresses and how to knit. With relatives living so close together on such a small island, we were never short of family celebrations. In fact, each Sunday was 'card playing day' between my mum, dad, Uncle Paul, and Aunt Evelyn. Uncle Fantin was not much of a card player and, instead, he would take me to their large garden where fruit trees flourished and he would show me how to encase the growing pear fruit in muslin pockets so the birds wouldn't eat them.

As I grew into my teen years, my father's emerging career made a big impression on me. In contrast, I felt disappointed in my mother's lack of self-confidence. I believed she had a lot of potential even though I knew that she lacked the opportunity for self-fulfillment in the culture she had been raised. Sometimes I feel that maybe I have been projecting my own goals and not hers. It's too late to ask her if she had been fulfilled as a wife and mother. Both my parents are now gone and many times I find myself saying,

"If I knew then what I know now, I would have been more understanding."

Chapter Four

Young Love

I met Tony Medati for the first time soon after I turned 13 and he was 16. He was a friend of our neighbor's sons across the street and their sister Tessie was my best friend. I began noticing him when he visited her brothers Joe and Louis.

When Tony was only 12 years old his father passed away. Tony had an older brother and sister. His sister Hilda had been working as a seamstress, but with the postwar conditions there had not been much demand for her skills. During the war she worked as a nurse's aid and helped move casualties of disaster emergencies. She eventually married a Scotsman and moved to Scotland, where she again was able to work as a nurse's aid, this time in a children's home. His brother Joe's interest had been in craft hobbies. He built all sorts of model airplanes, from ones that were powered simply with twisted rubber bands to others that were radio controlled, and flew them in a nearby park. He constructed boats and cars from kits and even hand carved his own creations from balsa wood. He eventually got married and started a family and as conditions on the island improved, he opened up a hobby shop. Yet again, hobbies are not something people spend money on when there is dire need for more important things like food and shelter, so Joe's family finances were strained. At 16 Tony found himself the main caretaker of his widowed mother and earning money for her support took priority over his schooling.

The owner of the primary newspaper on the island, the *Times of Malta*, was Miss Strickland, a woman who was big and powerful in many ways. She was tall in stature and heavyset. Professionally, she controlled the news and had supported the war with Allied propaganda. She had a strong influence on the island and people in power did their best to stay in her good graces. Her newspaper reporters were the eyes and ears of the land and any scandal, personal or political would be quickly reported. She never married; the newspaper was her whole life. In spite of her apparent strong-handed manner she also had a benevolent side, one that included education and financial help for the underprivileged. Thus it happened that Tony qualified for one of her programs and he enrolled as an apprentice in the newspaper's accounts department. He became quite proficient with numbers and within a year advanced to full employment.

When I turned 15 I started to have an interest in boys, and Tony, who was now 18, would tease me by tugging at my hair as I passed by or bumping into me pretending he did not see me. I was enticed by his smile, his big brown eyes and dark wavy hair. I thought he looked like a young Tyrone Power, a handsome American actor very popular at the time.

My parents did not allow me to date anyone so we began to exchange notes. Soon our little notes evolved into long letters. One day I gave Tony one of my photos and at the edge of it he wrote, "I love you sweetie" and the date, "3rd August 1946." Then he turned it over and wrote, "She gave it to me, date of birth 24th March 1931. I have to wait two years and seven months from the above date to take her from my enemy's hands and be mine forever." I felt confused when he showed me what he had written. Even though my father had forbidden me to date Tony I did not consider him Tony's enemy. 'Enemy' seemed to me a harsh word, but when Tony kissed the photo, placed it in his wallet and tenderly looked back at me, I forgot about my father and I felt loved and flattered.

Our letters grew more passionate but to be honest, I hardly knew what passion was. I had never dated. It was more like fairytale longings, at least to me. I imagined having a house on an acre or two, complete with a white picket fence, children, dogs and horses. No one on the rocky island of Malta, aside from farmers, had more than an acre of land or a horse. My fantasies came from watching American movies and looking at American magazines that my father brought home after they had been discarded at the American Embassy.

Tony and I continued writing to each other on a regular basis for almost three years, sharing our dreams for a future together. One day I became more daring. In my letters I told him how I longed to hold him and kiss him and how his touch thrilled me. I had never really had any occasion to do either; the words were verbatim from songs I had heard on the American Forces Network's Hit Parade. Unfortunately my father found the letters and believed the worst. Both my parents were quite upset and suspected that somehow we had found ways to meet each other. Friends of the family and even a priest from our church congregation suggested to them that they should take me to places where I could meet others of my own age and hopefully that would make me forget all about Tony. I then realized that my parents were not only against my dating but particularly did not want me to date Tony because of his lack of schooling. On the small island people were very class conscious.

I remember the time my mother took me to a local teenage dance where she joined other mothers as a chaperon. Friends from my all-girl high school were there, and I also recognized some of the young men. I was invited to dance by a couple of them and I did. The music was supplied by a disc jockey. We danced to current Hit Parade music from the fast *In the Mood* to the slow and lovely *It's Magic* sung by Doris Day.

One of the young men told me that he knew a cousin of mine and then asked me why he hardly ever sees me there. I sadly told him how I was never allowed to go out alone, or even with friends, but only with older relatives. I enjoyed the music, the friends and the dancing, but my eyes were constantly searching the dance floor. It was about an hour into the dance when my heart fluttered as I saw Tony enter the hall. Unfortunately my mother saw him too and as the dance ended and my partner walked me back to her, she stood up from her chair, picked up her purse, grabbed my arm and announced, "We are leaving." She never took me to another local dance again.

The following February was Carnival time. I was almost 18 years old by now and my parents planned to take me to a costume ball. In Malta, Carnival is similar to events in Rio de Janeiro or New Orleans with parades, fancy costumes, dancing competitions, decorated floats and masked balls in the evening. The three-day event is an extravagant, fun filled and revel-making festivity prior to the beginning of Lent. In contrast, the following Lenten season is a time of fasting and penance in preparation for the celebration of Easter.

Instead of being happy and excited, I was petrified at the prospect of going to this dance. I could not forget what had happened at the previous dance and how humiliating it would be if Tony showed up and I would be dragged home again. Furthermore, this dance was being held at my father's upscale Men's Club. I did not know how to behave with this elite crowd. I felt shy and inexperienced. I overheard my mother tell one of her friends that she and dad were doing this for my sake, to get me to meet a better class of people. I then realized that this dance had been by invitation only, for members and friends of the Club. Tony would not be attending and worse still, all the girls most likely had dates for the evening. I might be the only girl unaccompanied by an escort. I did not want to go, but my parents insisted and bought me a Cinderella-like gown which I did not care for as I did not have any glass slippers and no way of meeting my prince.

The night of the dance I developed a terrible headache. Soon my heart started beating rapidly. I became nauseated and my father reluctantly sent me to bed. For all I know I might have had a wonderful time. Looking back, this was my first panic attack, from which I still occasionally suffer when I feel overwhelmed.

After further consideration and much discussion, my parents finally agreed to allow Tony and me to date. Dating meant simply going to a movie together on weekends with a curfew of 9 p.m., no exceptions. The movies started at 5 p.m. and 7 p.m., except we rarely went to the earlier show since my mother insisted we have afternoon tea and sandwiches with the family at that time. We would then go to the 7 p.m. movie but then had to leave the theater before the movie ended to be home by curfew. In retrospect, I can hardly believe I had to do this, but I was so afraid that if I got home later than 9 p.m. I would again be forbidden to go out with my sweetheart.

Conditions seemed so bad, so strict, and so unrealistic that one day Tony and I decided that I should run away from home. Now this was a major yet naive undertaking. First, there was nowhere to go or to hide on this small island and, second, we had no idea what we would do. It was almost comical because we had no car, no money and no definite plans, just a stubborn rebellion against the way things were. Considering my strict upbringing, this was also a step that should have terrified me, but what I remember is an experience of daring excitement.

It was about two in the afternoon when Tony came to my house. I had gathered some clothes and underwear in a small suitcase, opened the front door and joined him. My mother saw me leaving the house and came running to the door. Tony and I sped down the street, running as fast as we could and to this day I can almost hear my mother yelling hysterically after me. She must have been so scared, so horrified. She surely would telephone my father at his office. We had taken a bus three miles to the next town of Valetta, when we saw him drive by looking for us. How it must have pained my parents. How they must have worried. I had been oblivious to all of that, then.

We walked for miles it seemed, constantly watching for any sign of my father. By late evening, after having something to eat and not knowing what to do next we returned to Tony's home back in Sliema where he still lived with his widowed mother, like all unmarried children did at the time.

Evidently my parents had contacted her because when we arrived she was in an uproar, angry with her son for taking me away from my home. She called my parents to let them know we were there and that they could come and pick me up. For the first time I began to worry about the consequences of what we had done. I felt sure that my father would give me a good spanking and I got scared. I ran up to the roof of the house, which was accessible from inside via a spiral staircase, similar to most houses in Europe. I hid in the shadows and began contemplating what I would do if they came after me. Horrible thoughts crossed my mind. I searched for ways to climb down without going back into the house. Large drainage pipes were anchored to the outside walls to drain rain water from the roof down to the patio area below, but the house was three stories high and as I looked down I felt dizzy, so that was not an option.

To my great relief Tony came to the roof looking for me. He told me that my parents were downstairs, that they had paid a visit to the parish priest of our church and that they had agreed to let us become *engaged!* They also promised to forgive our little escapade and not punish me.

I was skeptical, but when they kept their word I began to understand how afraid they must have been.

What gave me my rebellious trait? Was it my parents' severe curfew, the strict rules of my upbringing, the effects of the war? They had meant to protect me, to shield me from making mistakes, yet their rigid rules also kept me from meeting new people and learning to socialize. I had lots of friends in school my own age, but I had not been allowed to go places with them after school. I longed for attention, so when Tony playfully flirted with me, I eagerly responded.

I do not know where I got the courage that day. I guess something within me needed to be expressed. This episode imprinted in me a sense of achievement, that I could change things if I tried. The end result might not always be what I had hoped, but my self-esteem ignited and later on in my life, this persistence and my searching for alternate ways to deal with dilemmas proved to be a lifesaver. As I once read, "You cannot escape life by not living it. One has to give it one's all."

Allowing us to get engaged and start planning a wedding date was my parents' way of dealing with the possibility that I may otherwise run away again or their fear that I may even become pregnant, something I would never have done. Mum and Dad had raised me in the only way they knew how. I am sure they believed I could marry "better." They might have been right, but they had never allowed me the opportunities to make other decisions, so I fell in love with a neighborhood boy, who showed me affection and persisted in spite of all their restrictions. Tony and I happily began planning for our wedding day.

Chapter Five

Beginning Dreams

My father had always been a radio aficionado. We had mantel radios, table radios, freestanding radios, shortwave and longwave. My father's radios had very powerful reception that allowed us to pick up a variety of broadcasts. As a teenager at the end of WWII, I listened to "Amos and Andy," "Boston Blackie," "The Shadow," "Jigs and Maggie," "Baby Snooks," "The Hit Parade" and other programs that the American Armed Forces Network broadcasted from Stuttgart Germany. I soon became the envy of my school friends. I also began to love American ways, their comedies, their mystery stories and their music. My father, being brought up on 'proper English,' did not always understand the American slang of some of these programs. Many evenings I had my ears glued to the radio and it was my joy to later repeat the humor and 'translate' it for my father and we would laugh together.

My special enjoyment was listening to a detective story called "Box 13" which featured Alan Ladd. I decided to write to him in Hollywood, telling him how much I liked the program. Imagine my astonishment when I received back two 8x10 portrait photographs signed and addressed to me "with love." Also enclosed was a letter inquiring how on earth I could hear the program on my island and from where was it being broadcast? I wrote back and explained that it was being broadcast from Germany and that we had powerful radio reception. Apparently they had not been aware that we could pick up their signal on the island.

My father's connections at the American Embassy in Malta allowed him to acquire their discarded publication issues. I would eagerly read and reread these American magazines including *Life* and *Look*. All the articles and pictures became etched in my memory, including the advertisements for new washing machines, televisions and refrigerators; none of which were available in Malta at the time. I slowly but surely came to love America and realized that this was where I wanted to live.

American movies also encouraged my fondness for the United States. MGM had musicals and Warner Bros. offered suspense and mystery stories. I loved to watch movies featuring Esther Williams performing her synchronized swimming underwater. The beautiful sounds of the Big Band orchestras and the lavish houses with their lush gardens and Art Deco décor thrilled me. The movies, the advertising and the songs on the radio all helped to reinforce my desire to come to America.

Jobs were plentiful in the U.S. and the economy was booming. New houses were being built in America for returning servicemen. At the same time, the scars of war were still very obvious on Malta. Many of the houses, offices churches and government buildings were in a state of rubble. The few farming areas on the island's rocky plateau were full of holes left gaping as a hungry bird's mouth and dust and ash covered the pot-holed streets. The young people now growing up into adulthood could not find any employment and housing became a victim of the black market where one had to pay a bribe to get referral to a house or apartment that might become available.

The call for emigration was like the sound of a siren blowing in the wind on Calypso Island, only this time the entreaty was *away from the island*. The continuous flow of the American magazines exposed me to panoramas and vistas I had never seen. By war's end my beautiful semi-tropical island was a devastated blend of shambles and stood like an empty shell.

I felt like Cinderella *before* her life was transformed by meeting her prince. We still washed by hand with a scrubboard in a tub over a gasoline stove. We shopped for food on a daily basis, as we had no way to keep the food cold. We cooked whatever we could buy that had not become moldy, wilted or foul. Store supplies were minimal. We sewed our own clothes and knitted our own sweaters. A government issue of food and clothing stamps provided meager yet much needed rations.

Our strategic island had been the bulwark of the allies and we had helped win the war, but now trying to rebuild our lives and facing the realities of the devastation suddenly made emigration a powerful option. I was fourteen when the war ended and my imagination had sparked up a teen's folly and a teen's daring hopes. Through the movies and the magazines I had seen flourishing America. In every article and advertisement I saw a smiling happy woman, man or child with glistening teeth, hair in glorious colors and beautiful rosy cheeks. I believed America must be heaven on earth.

In the next four years I had attended school and watched my island slowly start to repair itself. I fell in love and intensified my dreams of immigrating to my fantasy-land thousands of miles away, even though it was considered a disgrace for a daughter to leave her family and country and move to a faraway land. My parents, though unhappy about my upcoming marriage to Tony, understood that our future in Malta looked dim. While Tony had a solid job at the *Times of Malta*, housing was still scarce. Under the circumstances, and the condition that the island was in, they reluctantly agreed that emigration gave us a chance for a better life.

I was glad to discover that Tony had been as eager as I to emigrate; however, we soon learned that immigration quotas to America were only allotted in proportion to the population of the country of birth and because Malta was so small, we would have a delay of almost ten years before our number even came up.

Canada and Australia both needed people to populate and work their lands. My husband-to-be and I applied for immigration to Canada where we decided to live until granted the opportunity to move to the United States. Canada desired English-speaking immigrants who like Canadians, were also British Subjects. Our application to migrate was immediately granted and after filing the necessary papers and passing our physical exams we were given our papers to enter Canada.

When Tony and I were finally married on March 10, 1951, the date happened to be during Lenten season. Our church did not usually conduct wedding ceremonies at this solemn time, but the Bishop gave us a special dispensation since Tony had to leave for Canada in eight days. My parents did not want us to have a big celebration during this pre-Easter fasting period so we settled for a small reception at my parents' home. It turned out to be a mixture of congratulations for our union and sad commentary regarding our leaving the island, family and friends.

To the very end my parents continued to discourage our union and had many times made derogatory remarks that hurt to this day. On one occasion, Tony had sent me flowers that I displayed proudly in the center of our dining room table. When my father came home and noticed my beautiful bouquet, he asked my mother who sent them to him. He assumed they were for him because many times he received tokens of thanks for projects he had completed. When my mother replied,

"They belong to Alice, Tony sent them." My father laughed out loud and asked,

"What are they for?"

Had he forgotten how he felt when he was courting mom? I looked at the flowers lovingly, but somehow they seemed to have lost their glorious bloom.

A week before our wedding Tony and I had seen the movie 'Father of the Bride' with Spencer Tracy and Elizabeth Taylor. I really enjoyed watching it and particularly took notice of how, after the wedding reception, the bride and groom ran happily to their waiting car while their parents and guests showered them with rice, threw kisses and called out their best wishes. Our wedding day was approaching and my eyes filled with tears as I became fully aware of how different ours was going to be. We were not going away to a romantic honeymoon destination. Tony would be leaving for Canada in just eight days and our parents were not enthusiastically cheering for us. I clutched Tony's hand and buried my head in his shoulder and silently sobbed. My head slipped to his chest and I could hear and feel his heart beating. Its steady rhythm and his warmth consoled me. He held me tight as he caressed my face and said,

"Our time will come. The important thing is that we are getting married. We are going to Canada and then to America, remember that."

He wiped my tears away, then realizing that we had to hurry home because of my curfew, we soon left the theater. We were both quiet in our own thoughts as we hastened our steps.

As planned our wedding reception was a small party at my parents' home. The event included a three-tier cake, hors d'oeuvres, finger sandwiches, tarts, and numerous delicate sweets. We also had an open bar for our guests. Music played via gramophone and for our wedding song we chose *It Had to Be You.* This song was first published in 1924 by Isham Jones and the lyrics were by Gus Kahn, moreover, in 1951 the year of our marriage, Danny Thomas had sung it in the movie *I'll See You in My Dreams* and it had become a wedding favorite.

The guests were mostly relatives and close friends of my parents. My father's prestigious position guaranteed many acquaintances, some in high places, so I do not doubt that Lent gave my parents a good excuse to keep my wedding more intimate and private. Considering that they were not happy with my marriage to Tony and regretting that we were leaving the island even more, I felt grateful that at least they had provided us with a celebratory wedding reception.

Our short honeymoon was to be spent at a local hotel on Savoy Hill, fittingly named The Savoy Hotel. As we prepared to leave the reception we went upstairs to change out of our formal attire. I was to wear a blue two-piece wool outfit consisting of a dress and jacket made by a neighborhood seamstress, pearl-gray gloves and shoes with a matching bag. In my jacket lapel I had pinned a pearl and gold brooch that my mother had loaned me for the occasion. Tony had a new dark blue suit.

My mother had placed Tony's clothes in her bedroom upstairs and mine in another room across a long hall overlooking the spiral staircase. As I tried to zip up the back of my dress I found out that I could not reach far enough to close it so I ran across the hall to ask Tony to help me with the zipper. I suddenly heard mother's footsteps coming up the stairs. I got flushed and hurriedly went back to my room, afraid of being caught in the same room with Tony. We were married now, but the fear of my mother suspecting that we might be doing something wrong was hard to overcome, at least not in one day. She helped me with the dress and my heart calmed from its pounding excitement. I never did find out why my mother came upstairs in the first place. I have a suspicion that she would have liked to have a mother-daughter talk with me yet did not know what to say. Anyway it was a little too late.

We finished dressing and Tony and I started down the staircase together. I could see the smiling faces of our guests looking up with anticipation. Filled with bliss, we rushed down the rest of the steps and turned right towards the front door. The guests joyfully pelted us with rice. We happily waved at them, but before we could even reach the front door my mother's voice bellowed from the back of the room,

"Are you leaving without saying goodbye to me?"

I froze in my tracks. I had thought that she would come and say goodbye to me… that is what Elizabeth Taylor's mother had done in the movie. The guests stopped throwing rice, and for what seemed to be an eternity, we stood silently together in the foyer. I felt as if I had turned to stone. Finally, I regained my composure and with all the strength I could muster I turned back, walked among the guests to the back of the room and gave my mother a hug and a kiss. As I returned to Tony, the guests cheered and threw rice again, but by then I was numb. My mother had managed to spoil my happiest day and punish me for leaving, in the only way she knew how, by creating an awkward and embarrassing final moment and stealing the wind from my sails.

During these precious seven days of our honeymoon, we were invited to dinner at several relatives' houses and especially to my parents and to Tony's mother's. The shadow of our upcoming departure hung over our heads like a dark cloud and everywhere we went a sense of sadness seemed to precede us. We all just made small talk, but never discussed our impending move to Canada. It was too heavy a subject for conversation. Unlike a vacation holiday abroad, we were embarking on a permanent journey to the unknown. Tony had to leave before me to seek accommodations, find a job and make preparations for my arrival.

Our honeymoon week was full of apprehension and excitement for both of us. This was the beginning of our new life together and a chance at a very different kind of life. We talked about having a ranch, a horse and even the white picket fence, things we had read about in magazines. We were both full of hopes and expectations. After all,

Canada was so much bigger than our tiny island and more importantly, close to the United States. We were getting nearer to our dream.

I had never held a job or had any money of my own. Our cash wedding gifts were my first taste of independence - financial or otherwise. And so it was that my mother had selected my wedding trousseau including nightwear and undies. Their styling can be described as *practical*. She had chosen a flannel pair of pajamas for me (with top and bottom) that would keep me warm in the much colder Canadian climate. They would also stand in as a nice cover-up en route, during my travel adventure. This nightwear was certainly not what I would have liked for my romantic wedding night.

I was very shy, unsophisticated and inhibited that night and did not know much what to expect. Although Tony and I both had strong feelings for each other and had done some general petting, we had never made love. We even took turns taking a shower. Seeing movies today of people jumping naked into bed before they are married or with a near-complete stranger, makes me laugh at our wedding day naiveté. Everything was guesswork. I was about to turn twenty, but I had constrained and hidden emotions demanded by my strict upbringing, our culture and our religion where we were taught that every emerging normal sensual feeling was considered a sin, whether acted upon or not. I doubt that all the teenagers on the island followed these strident rules, although most of my peers did and fears of going to hell were stronger than fears of getting pregnant. What I could never understand was why, when a boy strayed from the right path, it was said he was "sowing his wild oats," while if a girl made a mistake and got pregnant she was chastised and found it very difficult to then find a young man willing to marry her.

Of course this was almost 60 years ago (late 1940's early1950's) and prior to the sexual revolution when movies showed only people kissing and then the picture would turn to *rushing waves*. On TV Lucy and Desi slept in separate beds. Things have changed in many ways since then.

My mother had never talked to me about sex and my girlfriends were not any more knowledgeable about the subject. I am sure that Tony had talked with his pals, but even his impression was to get married with the goal to start a family. Culturally, we were still very Victorian, especially among the so-called finer classes. We were both shy and inexperienced at exploring each other sensually. Our lovemaking was strictly in the missionary position. Physically this might have left a lot to be desired had we known better, but our hearts were full of love for each other and our spiritual union was complete.

When the day came for Tony to depart for Canada I experienced feelings of foreboding mixed with exhilaration. He was leaving on the Greek ship the *Neptunia*, which would take 11 days to reach New York and then he would have to take the train to Toronto, Canada. He was leaving me to go thousands of miles away, but it also meant that I would be joining him soon, to start our new life together. My father, his mother and all our brothers and sisters joined me at the pier to wave goodbye. It was evening when the ship set sail and the blue sky had become quite overcast. Darker clouds were gathering in the distance adding to the gloominess in my heart, and when at last the ship left and I could see it no more, I went back to my parents' home. My mother had not come to the peer and had not even offered one word of consolation. I had my separate bed, however not my own room. I had always shared a room with my two brothers. The bedroom was large and three single beds fitted easily. I took to bed with me one of Tony's shirts. I wanted to feel his warmth, wanted to imagine him close to me and inhale his scent. My father entered the room to say goodnight and noticed it. He laughed... I cried.

A week later, on March 24th, I celebrated my 20th birthday by reading and rereading Tony's first letter mailed to me from the ship as it was nearing Halifax, Canada. He reminisced about our week as husband and wife and promised to send for me as soon as he could.

I spent the following month saying goodbye to my friends and relatives. Aunt Lola, my father's sister, met me at the market one day and frankly asked,

"Are you pregnant?" I was so startled that for a moment I could not find my tongue. Even my mother had not asked me this.

"No-o" I stammered, without any elaboration.

"Why not?" she insisted, "Is anything wrong?"

To my embarrassment I found myself explaining everything and hating her inquisitiveness and soon waved her goodbye.

In Malta at the time, when young women got married they pretty soon found themselves pregnant. The fact that Tony and I would be separated for an undetermined length of time would have been reason enough for us to prevent conception, but I knew nothing about contraception. Tony might have had an idea, still it was never a topic of discussion and our church forbade contraception anyway.

Possibly Aunt Lola's question was normal and to be expected, but I had been nervous and a little ashamed to admit that I was not pregnant. Soon I began to wonder and pray that "nothing was wrong" as she put it. I became more eager than ever to get to Canada and prove to them and to myself that all was well indeed.

A few more weeks went by and Tony's letters arrived on a regular basis. He had found a job at Werner's Aluminum, in the City of Oshawa, thirty miles east of Toronto, where they made those 1950's Formica dinette sets. He had never done any manual labor before, but the accounting departments in Canada worked with dollars and cents, not with pounds, shillings and pence like in Malta so he had not tried for an office job. He had then filed the necessary papers for me to join him.

"Do not worry," he explained, "any job will do to get you here."

My father provided me with a large trunk and I started packing my wedding gifts. The trunk was made of wood and had leather straps encircling it with metal locks to close it tight. It measured 2 ft. wide by 3 ft. high and 4 ft. long yet I soon feared that I would not have enough space for everything until a friend who was watching me pack pots and pans and a teakettle, started to laugh,

"Take those things back out," she advised, "don't you think they have pots and pans in Canada?"

She was right of course, and as I removed them I found more room for our more appropriate wedding gifts. Among my presents were silk bedspreads, towels and table linens. Some had fine handmade lace embroidery and others were beautifully monogrammed; definitely more important to take with me than kitchen utensils.

When the day of my departure arrived, mother again did not come to the pier. She claimed that she was too distraught and started crying, then said,

"You will soon forget all about me."

This time I did not feel guilty. My excitement and my happiness at the thought that I will soon be with Tony again overcame any other emotion. I had no intention of forgetting all about my mother. I was raised to respect her; however, her coldness and apparent inability to show love saddened me. I knew she loved me and that it must have pained her to see me go, but I had determined that nothing and no one was going to spoil this day for me. I wish she were still alive so that I could tell her that I loved her and how I had wished that she had sent me away with her blessings, not with her resentment. I know now that she did not realize what she was doing, only that she felt hurt and blamed me because I was the one leaving.

My father, my Aunt Evelyn, my brothers and sister and Tony's mother and sister all came to bid me farewell. I sailed on the Greek ship the *Nea Hellas*. It was larger than the *Neptunia* that Tony had sailed on. I was among other immigrants who were also going to Canada to meet up with their husbands. We all gathered on the deck to watch the island get smaller and smaller until we could see it no more. I had a lot of mixed emotions. I was not only leaving my mother behind but also my whole family and all my friends. We all promised to write to each other and that I would send a wire home as soon as I arrived in Canada.

Leaving my family was not as devastating as I thought it would be. My two brothers did not say much about my departure, yet deep in my heart I knew that they would miss me and I would miss them. They were still attending high school and my older brother Ronnie was also taking classes in accounting, his chosen profession. My brother Joe was only 15 and I probably felt more of a kinship towards him, as he had been the one who I could bribe to clean the table and wash the dishes for me while I recounted for him the movie I had seen the day before. My younger sister Marlene was almost 12 years old and quite happy that my leaving resulted in me giving her my dolls, my play china tea set and other childhood keepsakes including my favorite teddy bear. Soon I began to feel the enthusiasm and excitement for the whole adventure ahead.

I had been so restricted, hardly ever allowed to leave my parents' sight, and now, here I was sailing thousands of miles away to a different land and starting a new life with my beloved husband, leaving my world behind and embarking on an incomprehensible journey. The thought of leaving my family, the isolation I might encounter and the hardships I could be facing did not penetrate my immature mind. I found myself finally free to be me… or so I thought.

Chapter Six

New Life in Canada

The *Nea Hellas* was an immense and beautiful Greek ship with numerous decks. It had ballrooms, big band orchestras, movie theatres, swimming pools, boutiques, bars and luxurious massage salons. The Canadian government was sponsoring the immigration program and paid for my passage as well as my husband's. First-class passengers occupied the topmost decks; unfortunately as immigrants, we were allocated to the steerage section in the bottom deck. The crew's sleeping quarters and the kitchens were also located here. There were four bunk beds in each tiny cabin, two on either side of the room with a very narrow space in between. Each room also had a sink, though the toilets and showers were down the hallway and shared with the other cabins. The only place for our luggage was under the beds. Families that came together were assigned to a room, but single men and women were on different sides of the ship and shared a room with others.

When I embarked I had not known the three other women who shared my cabin, except that they were also young newlyweds who were going to Canada to join their husbands. During the voyage I got to learn a little about them, but aside from getting together for our meals, we were individually absorbed in our own private thoughts. While I was traveling alone, the three other women were from the same village and had known each other for some time. I often went out by myself to explore other areas of the ship or just to watch the waves roll by and wonder what the future held in store. I was on my way to a new country and that filled me with awe.

As we crossed the Mediterranean Sea all appeared calm, but as we reached Gibraltar, the gateway to the Atlantic Ocean, the steward came to our cabin and sealed shut the portholes with a strong rubber-edged cover. That is when my roommates and I realized that our cabin was going to be below sea level as we hit the rough waters. Soon moisture seeped in under the beds and we had to raise our luggage to the foot of our bunks.

The voyage to Canada via New York took eleven days. The ocean became quite rough at times with tables swaying and food being spilled. Actually the tables were bolted down, it was the ship that swayed. Our stomachs did not easily conform to the feel of the deck moving under our feet. A crew member suggested that we keep our eyes focused on the horizon, but that did not help much and many of us lost our breakfasts and avoided lunch and dinner if the sea was still rough.

Immigrants were only allowed up to the first deck above sea level. We could hear the music and laughter coming from the upper decks. The stairs leading to the top floors only had a rope across them, nevertheless stewards were on the lookout for strays.

On one lucky occasion the rope was down and I managed to sneak to an upper deck. It was evening and I could see people dancing in the large rooms. Balls of light sparkled on the ceiling and the sound of mellow music drifted out to the deck. Men in striking formal attire and women in luxurious long gowns twirled and laughed and enjoyed the glitter. I had never been exposed to such high glamour before. A steward saw me at the doorway but chose to say nothing. Other stewards were occupied carrying trays with drinks and catering to this elite crowd. After a while as I watched in awe, a young man came towards me and asked me if I wanted to dance. I stood there petrified, my face flushed, and I felt as if I was going to faint. I shook my head and managed to mumble,

"No thank you."

I looked down at my flat shoes, my short skirt and plain blouse and became very uncomfortable. I was amazed that anyone from this sophisticated group had actually paid attention to me. In retrospect, I think that he had only seen me as a young 20-year-old woman filled with wonder and had not even noticed my clothes. The steward did not have to ask me to leave, as I knew that I did not fit in. I slowly edged out of the room and made my way back to the lower decks.

During the early morning hours the smells from the kitchen and the odors from the smoke stacks made for a sickening duo. I would bathe and hurry up the stairs to the first open deck to ease my discomfort with the fresh air. Most of the days were spent playing cards with fellow immigrants and exchanging ideas at what awaited us. We dreamed of a life away from our devastated yet beloved homeland and tried to assure each other that things were bound to be better than the war-ravaged conditions we had left behind.

At night it was simply magic standing on deck with the stars gleaming above and the soothing sound of the sea parting as the ship pushed its way across the ocean. I could see the lights from the decks above shimmering below. Time stood still. It seemed as if I was in a fantasyland, slowly drifting between two worlds. I missed my husband the most at those romantic times and wished he could have been with me.

After passing Gibraltar we saw nothing but ocean water until about nine days later when we finally came close to Nova Scotia, Canada. It was the same area where the Titanic had tragically sunk. The land appeared very desolate and surreal with large pine trees engulfed in fog. I wondered if all of Canada was like that, noting an overpowering difference from my sub-tropical island. It had been my first time away from home and I suddenly felt overcome with apprehension at the reality of this large land that was unknown to me.

We went on to New York the next day where we were to take a train to Toronto, the capital city of Ontario, Canada. The revered Statue of Liberty dominated the harbor just as I had seen it in magazines. The early afternoon sun filtered through the mist and my eyes filled with tears of joy. My heart began to beat hard and fast and my anticipation soared. Tony sent me a wire stating that although he could not meet me in New York, he would be waiting for me at the station in Toronto. I was very disappointed.

We went through customs easily since most of us on the ship were not U.S. bound but just passing through. The customs officers stamped our passports and casually checked our luggage. They asked us a few simple questions and were relieved that we could speak English. They then guided us towards the street and a fellow passenger helped us across the way to the train station. I arranged for my trunk to be delivered to Toronto via freight.

By the time I stepped out of the U.S. Customs Building the sun had set and the bright lights of the street were dazzling. I looked around me in disbelief; the skyscrapers, the big stores, the cafes, the neon signs, the traffic and the noise all were enough to distract my fears as my travel companions and I made our way to New York Central Station. This was America, the land of my dreams, the place I really wanted to be. I had glimpsed what I believed to be paradise on earth and as I climbed the train taking me to Canada I prayed that I would some day be able to return and stay.

We left New York that evening, traveling throughout the night, and arrived in Toronto in the early morning. I had been too nervous, too excited and too curious to sleep so by the time we arrived I was physically exhausted. My passport and papers were checked as we arrived in Toronto and I was admitted into the country and into my husband's awaiting arms.

I had known him since I was 13 and I had not seen him since he had left Malta three months earlier. We hugged and kissed and we were thrilled that at last we were together in this new land. I was tired and bewildered at my experiences of the past weeks. I was not prepared for his reaction when I innocently mentioned to him that a young man who was with us on the ship and who had been to Malta on vacation had thankfully helped me through the maze of U.S. customs and had directed me to the train station. He had also assisted me with the transfer and shipping of my trunk to Toronto. In a jealous overreaction my husband removed his wedding band from his finger and stuffed it in his pocket. What had happened? What did I do? In my naive confusion I just sat there and silently cried.

Tony took me for breakfast at the train cafeteria. My trunk would not arrive for two weeks, so after eating we took the bus to Oshawa, thirty miles east of Toronto, where Tony had rented two rooms in a family home. The episode at the train station was not mentioned again. Tony had bought a bedroom set; one dollar down and one dollar a week. In those days more business was transacted with cash rather than by check and very few people even had a credit card.

Our two-room living quarters were upstairs next to a shared bathroom. Our bedroom furniture filled one room and the second room was empty. Apparently my husband had been sleeping in but eating out. Of course I had not expected much more as he had only been in this new country for three months.

We made love that night and I happily slept in my husband's arms well into the next morning. That day we bought an icebox, a hotplate, a few dishes and some pots and pans and set up a make-shift kitchen in the second room. I had never cooked before so our first meals at home were mostly fried eggs and fried potatoes. I cabled my parents to let them know that I had arrived safely and later wrote a long letter telling them of my experiences and begging my mother for recipes! A couple of weeks later we were notified to go to Toronto for a customs inspection of my trunk that had arrived at the station.

Weeks earlier, U.S. Customs in New York had opened only several items in my trunk when they came across a large wooden box that my father had fastened with screws. They asked me what was in it and I explained that it contained a bust of Jesus secured to a wooden plaque. My father had wrapped a blanket around it and secured it tightly for protection against breakage. It had been a wedding present from Tony's mother. The customs officer smiled and said,

"I am not going to open it, say a prayer for me when you get to Canada."

I thought that was so sweet. Also he probably did not want to take out all the screws. Similarly, now in Toronto, when we went to pick up my trunk, the customs officer checked everything and then also asked me what was in the box that was screwed shut. I naively replied,

"They did not open it in New York."

In an authoritarian voice he declared,

"This is Canada," and proceeded to unscrew the box completely which took him quite some time. When the trunk arrived at our apartment via truck delivery, we set it in the other room and used it as our dining table.

A month after I arrived in Canada I began to feel queasy and I thought it was all the fried eggs and potatoes that we had been eating;

however, a medical check-up proved that I was pregnant. We were absolutely thrilled with the news.

Remembering my husband's tantrum when I first arrived, I desperately prayed that our baby would be carried the full term so that Tony will not imagine any wrongdoing on my part.

Our first summer in Canada was delightful. We picnicked in the park and spent weekends strolling by Lake Ontario that bordered our city of Oshawa. The lake was too cold to swim in and did not compare well to the Mediterranean Sea, but we were on an adventure, starting a new family in this wondrous land and our enthusiasm made most things appear somewhat more beautiful than they really were.

We were overjoyed to find the streets lined with lush trees and green lawns in front of houses. In contrast Malta was a sub-tropical rocky island and the front of the house structures reached all the way to the sidewalk; yet many had small gardens in the backyard including fruit-bearing trees such as oranges and pears and also grapevines. In our garden, we had even had a large banana tree which required lots of water. I remember my father had creatively hooked up a pipe to the bathroom and rigged it so that the bath water would empty in the banana soil. To our amazement it had flourished and we supplied bananas to all our neighbors.

Flowers have always been revered on Malta and many people grew geraniums in planters located near front doors, on windows sills and on balconies. Colorful Bougainvillea often climbs the outside of houses and borders the garden walls in the back. It makes a beautiful and colorful contrast against the stark, white stone walls. In this new country, we now enjoyed the burst of color from an array of brilliant tulips and vivid native flowers.

The difference in culture and overall way of life between the two countries was also very evident. In Malta things were very tough immediately following the war. A young couple starting life together faced the harsh reality of damaged buildings and scarce, expensive food. It had been a blessing for us to be able to immigrate to an expanding country offering jobs and without the scars of war.

However, coming from a culture dominated by strong religion, education and the opera, to a settlement of new immigrants from different parts of the world, was a lesson in adaptation. I wanted to assimilate to feel at home in my surroundings. I tried to imitate Canadian people I met and for the first time in my life I dressed in jeans, listened to country music and shopped in local stores downtown. On Sundays though, I put on a dress, high heels, hat and gloves and my husband wore a suit because, for us, this was still the proper way to visit God's house. During the week I again changed into jeans, shirt, socks and tennis shoes. Sometimes I even went out with curlers in my hair because that is what the neighborhood women did. I thought all Canadians were like that and it would be many years before I had occasion to meet a higher class of people. I was an immigrant myself, struggling to save money and living in the poor side of town. Many times I missed home, especially the good times before the war, and I still often wondered what the future held for us.

When autumn arrived and the trees took on red, orange and yellow hues we saw it as a wonderland experience. This rainbow of warm colored leaves lasted about a month and then I noticed that the foliage began to fall off leaving the branches barren and soulful looking. This too was new to us and I loved walking with my shoes buried under two or three inches of leaves and hearing the crunch beneath my feet while the crisp air cooled my face and hands. My cheeks turned deep red against the icy rain that at times seemed to prick my skin even while it caressed it with its wetness. A gush of occasional chilly wind felt invigorating and walking at sunset, bundled in a warm wool coat and scarf, was exhilarating.

It was Canada's harsh winters that clouded my passion. By January the icy rain had turned to cold wet snow and the freezing wind to a bone-chilling and numbing ache. We had no car and our old winter clothes were inappropriate for this severe inclement weather. Whenever I left the comfort of our warm rooms and ventured outside, the cold air made my eyes tear and icicles formed on my eyelashes. Sniffles sometimes turned into nosebleeds and my hands and feet felt numb. As January turned into February the air in our rooms became stale and stuffy, sealed in with storm windows and storm doors. Waiting at the bus stop became intolerable and by the time I did some shopping and returned home, the beautiful snowflakes I had previously admired in November had become dirty slush. I am sure that if we had better clothes and a car, our experience would not have been so bleak. As it was, my first winter in Canada fanned my desire to move to a warmer and more familiar climate although the reality of going to California was still only a dream then.

Canada's worst winter month is February and by that time I was eight months pregnant. The temperature had dipped to six degrees below zero Fahrenheit and the winds blew without mercy. I remember watching a TV show called *Sergeant Preston of the Yukon*. It featured the work of the Canadian Mounted Police in the vast desolate area of the Northern Territories. As I looked out the windows of our two-room apartment on Bloor Street in Oshawa, I could see huge snowdrifts being blown and piled high against the top of six-foot fences. This might not be the Yukon Territory, but to me it was as close to the North Pole as I ever wanted to be. Houses with one foot of snow on their roofs were bellowing smoke from their chimneys. Condensation decorated the windowpanes with frost as the cold air tried to penetrate into the warm rooms inside. I did not dare step outside alone and I felt sorry for my husband who had to take a bus to and from work each day.

One particular Sunday with snow on the ground and dark clouds filling the sky, my husband and I walked to church, about a mile from our apartment, as we usually did each week. The service lasted about an hour and on returning outside we found that new snow had started to softly fall. We did not yet know anybody at the congregation and since we did not even think about spending money on a taxicab, we started walking back home.

As we trudged on our way, the wind began to pick up and we each tried hard to keep our nose and mouth covered with our gloved hands. Soon my fingers began to get numb and I walked with my head down so the snowflakes did not hit my face, especially my eyes.

My unborn baby seemed to react to the cold as I felt him roll around in my extended abdomen, the only part of my body that felt alive. Feeling the baby move, I instinctively dropped my hands from my face, pulled my coat tight and cuddled my belly in reassurance. The baby's movements stopped and the heat from my abdomen radiated out to the rest of my body.

My feet stepped faster and faster towards our home and as we reached the door and entered into the warmth of our rooms, I flopped into the nearest chair in relief. Removing my wet gloves, my hands burned and ached as they started to regain circulation and my husband took off my boots and gently rubbed my feet. The baby did a full turn that seemed to say 'now I can stretch again' as his foot hit under my ribs and made me wince. Our landlady must have heard us come in and knowing my condition and our unfamiliarity with this climate, she came to our door with two small glasses of brandy. I gladly sipped the soothing liquor and felt it recharge my heartbeat and rekindle the blood back into my veins.

Our son was born two weeks later on March 10th 1952 on our first wedding anniversary! We named him Jesse, a Biblical name we had selected before we were married.

Chapter Seven

Growing Family

When Tony left Malta, Miss Strickland, his boss and owner of the *Times of Malta* newspaper, had given him an introductory letter to the editor of the *Toronto Star* in Canada. Despite her help and his acquired knowledge in accounts, Tony was still naive and unexposed to higher education and business etiquette. He had also seen many American movies while growing up, which had given him the wrong impression of lifestyles outside of Malta. While trying to assimilate into this new culture his erroneous assumptions proved to be his downfall. He was gullible enough to believe that the casual and sometimes uncouth behaviors that he saw on screen were true. He did not have enough time to grow and learn to differentiate between fiction and reality.

Soon after arriving in Canada, Tony had his interview with the *Toronto Star's* editor. While chewing gum he answered questions with 'yeah' instead of 'yes' and subsequently was not hired. Sad to say, Tony had only been trying his best to fit in, in the only way he knew how. It was a long time before he came to realize that movies were not something to be emulated or taken as representative of normal cultural behavior. He still had a lot to learn. It was many years later that I found this out because at the time he could not face telling me of his humiliation. Unfortunately even today, this is how people overseas sometimes identify Americans, by what they see in our movies and on TV.

Tony's first job in Canada had been at Werner's Aluminum Co. The job was hard and dirty; extruding the aluminum from forms while it was still hot and pliable. He would come home from work covered in shiny black aluminum dust. While at work, he wore goggles and a mask over his nose and mouth, but the rest of his face and hair were ingrained with soot and his hair would even glisten from the aluminum powder. Though we would laugh and say he looked like a raccoon, it was a rough and unhealthy start.

We saved our money and did without many things and within two years we managed to put a down payment on a small town house. It was located at 65 3ʳᵈ Ave. on the side of town amidst other immigrants of various nationalities. We enjoyed our very first home and were thrilled to be homeowners no matter how humble. However, we were new at home buying and it was only after we moved in that we unhappily realized we were situated between three factories. A shuttle train that linked them came down our street right past our front door.

Our son Jesse, by then two years old, was born with big blue eyes and curly blond hair. People used to look at him and ask me,

"What is HER name?" mistaking him for a girl.

It always intrigued me why a boy cannot be just as beautiful. I had not known what to expect at his birth. I needed the comfort of a mother or family member, yet they were all so far away. My husband had stayed by my side at the hospital, but when the birth was imminent the nurse wheeled me into the delivery room, and Tony was not allowed to follow. In the 50's most women in Malta still gave birth at home with the help of a midwife so I really missed having someone with me. I gave birth to our son after twelve hours of moderate labor. My pains were hard, but the worst thing was that I had no idea how much worse it could get before he would arrive, as this was my first child. I can honestly say that the joy of his birth made it all worthwhile.

Our second child, daughter Dianne, was born on March 27ᵗʰ 1954. We had hoped for March 10ᵗʰ again, but nature did not comply. She was a darling redhead with hazel/green eyes. Her bright hair stood straight up in the center of her head and I had to endure teasing that she looked like a Mohawk Indian. Her birth was easy. After being taken to the delivery room the nurses thought that the baby was not ready to make its appearance. They gave me a buzzer and left to tend to other patients advising me to buzz when I felt frequent contractions. I remember it was just after midnight. They had called my doctor at his home and were awaiting his arrival.

I had been lying on the delivery table with a large mirror and light shining above me while another mirror was beyond the foot of the table and slanted to show my pelvic area. I recall having a strong contraction and looking in the far mirror I could see that my baby's head was beginning to crown. I got so excited I completely forgot to push the buzzer! I would probably have delivered her all alone had not my doctor happened to enter the room just then. A nurse quickly placed an oxygen mask on my face and begged me not to push. A few seconds later I began to feel drowsy as ether was administered, still I could hear Dr. Townsend say the magic words,

"You have a lovely daughter."

He had also delivered our son. As this was my second child, I had known what to expect and had been much more relaxed.

Soon after, my husband was able to get a new job at General Motors. It was an immense manufacturing plant that gave Oshawa the nickname of 'Motor City.' At this factory they made Pontiacs and Chevrolets for the Canadian market. Oshawa was also the home of Colonel McLaughlin who operated a carriage manufacturing business until 1908, when Michigan-based Buick Motor Company began shipping unassembled Buicks for assembly and marketing in Canada under the McLaughlin name. The Mclaughlin Buick production lasted until WWII. His estate, filled with antiques and surrounded by extravagant beautiful gardens, became a historical museum and a tourist attraction.

Tony's work at G.M. was an improvement over the dirty job at the aluminum plant. While still a boring assembly job, it was much cleaner and offered better pay. He was a diligent hard-working employee and worked three different rotating shifts. I hated his night shift because I was left alone with our babies. So we got a German Shepard dog that slept by my bed. Every morning Rocky would go down the stairs and sit by the front door waiting for Tony's arrival. I could hear his tail thumping on the floor as soon as he heard Tony's key in the lock.

One day a strange thing happened. Tony was late coming home so I was looking out the window to see if he was nearby. There was a commotion up the street. I could see people running and I heard a man saying that there was an accident; that a man had been hit by a car. In sudden fear I grabbed my coat and, leaving the dog to guard the house, I ran up the street to where the crowd had gathered.

An ambulance had already arrived and as I pushed through the crowd I saw Tony lying on the ground in a pool of blood. I fell on my knees and picked up his hand; it was warm but limp. With tears streaming down my cheeks I prayed,

"God, don't take him away, he is all I've got. Please God I need a miracle."

As soon as I said that, I felt that I was not worthy of a miracle. I was asking for too much. Then as if someone was whispering in my ear I heard myself say,

"God make this a dream. Please make it a dream."

I then woke up! Tony was peacefully sleeping next to me and his warm hand was still in mine. Had it only been a bad dream, or had my prayers been answered? I want to believe they were.

Soon we began to consider buying a larger house in a better neighborhood, but then December came again and we knew that no matter where we moved to in Canada, we could not escape the cold and dreadful winters. This inspired me to write a letter to the American President Dwight D. Eisenhower telling him how much my family and I wanted to come to America.

Writing to the President did not have the result I had hoped it would. I did receive acknowledgement for my letter, signed by a White House staff person, which informed me that we had to wait for our quota number. Of course I had suspected that I might have been clutching at straws in a desperate attempt to speed up our application for an entry visa. The year was 1956 and the next two years went by uneventfully while we waited. My husband was then moved from the dreary assembly line to the accounting office when personnel learned that he had experience in the accounts department in Malta. Besides the new currency, the whole accounting system proved to be different, nevertheless Tony adjusted and clearly liked his new position. Happily it also meant the end of the three-shift hassle.

In 1959 we had another blessed event. Our daughter Mariane Therese was born on October 17. It had been five and a half years since Dianne was born and I had been really looking forward to having this new baby and I had an excellent pregnancy. Dianne had inherited her brother Jesse's crib, baby clothes and baby carriage, but this time I had everything new again for this expected 'bundle of joy.' Being older, I had become more mature and aware. I watched my weight, ate nutritious foods and even considered natural childbirth without medication. However, things did not go as planned. On the expected date of her arrival, I was in the kitchen making supper when my water broke and I started to hemorrhage. I had no warning and no labor pains. My husband helped me to the living room couch and immediately called my doctor. The doctor said he would send an ambulance and instructed me to stay off my feet. In retrospect, I now know that I then did the most stupid and naive thing I could have done.

Because of my strict etiquette, upbringing and my ignorance, when my husband informed me that an ambulance was on its way, I experienced embarrassment at being found bleeding on the couch… I got up, climbed upstairs to the bathroom, cleaned myself as best I could and then lay down on the bed. Tony did not stop me. The ambulance attendants now had to bring the gurney up the stairs, and secure me on it, and then balance and maneuver me back down the narrow staircase. How much easier and safer it would have been if I had stayed downstairs on the couch. Sometimes behavior is so ingrained in us that we do what we are used to doing even when it is not to our benefit. I am so thankful that this stupid act did not hurt our baby. Of course I want to believe that I have come a long way since then, still that is the way it was.

The ambulance rushed me to the hospital with sirens blaring. By the time we got there I had begun passing blood clots like pieces of liver. My doctor consulted with other doctors, listened to my baby's labored pulse and decided that I needed an urgent Cesarean section. Everything started happening so fast that I had no time to be afraid. I just kept praying that my baby would be all right.

My encounter with fear soon followed. As I was being wheeled to the operating room, a priest bent over me and asked me if I wanted to say my confession. I was taken aback and could only ask,

"Am I going to die?"

He tried to assure me that this was a routine offering for Catholics going into surgery. He then blessed me, but the panic stayed with me. The thought that I might die had not entered my mind before. As the anesthesia flowed into me and I began drifting off to sleep, I remember saying goodbye to my family, naming each by name and including my unborn child. Then I left everything in the hands of the Blessed Mother Mary.

When I awoke, I was extremely weak having lost a lot of blood, and then received two transfusions. My baby had been placed in a nursery-room incubator so I could not see her right away. I had a hard time believing that she had survived this arduous delivery and was in good health. Because of my physical condition and the added emotional stress of not seeing my baby, I went into shock. I began shaking and shivering. I remember nurses rushing to my bed to pile blankets and heating pads over me. My teeth were chattering so much that I feared biting my tongue. Soon I felt myself rising gently towards the ceiling. I could see myself in the bed below. I watched as my doctor entered the room and gave me some medication via injection. I seemed to float above it all. I remember I did not want to leave the room and that at one time I had reached the corner of the room and stayed there above the doorway. I heard the nurses calling my name and I sensed a need to go down and reenter my body. Back in bed, I again heard the nurses call my name, but I could not answer. My mind seemed strong and active as I struggled to talk. I kept telling myself,

Stay calm, you will soon wake up… and I suddenly did.

A nurse then brought in my little baby Mariane for me to see, still in the incubator, but at last I could believe that she was well and my heart experienced peace. She had dark hair and big brown eyes and she was absolutely beautiful.

Chapter Eight

Happy Times – Sad Times

We were very happy in our marriage. We owned our humble home, had three lovely children, a family dog and even a white picket fence. Tony was very industrious and loved working around the house. He had replaced the kitchen floor, rebuilt the patio railing, designed a TV cabinet and constructed a coffee table for the living room. His hobbies included making radio control airplanes and flying them in the park and building a large model train layout in the basement for our son, complete with mountains, forests and villages. He was also a master at carving galleon ship models from balsa wood and building all the ship's finery by hand with objects found around the house. Popsicle sticks became the plank decking and window blinds were turned into sails. Old lipstick holders, which at that time were made of metal, became deck guns. His name was in the local paper for winning a trophy cup for his model of the *Santa Maria*, Columbus's ship. Later he made the much larger *U.S. Constitution* model, which required very intricate rigging.

He continued to work at General Motors while taking a correspondence course in Commercial Art. We were still debating on whether to buy a bigger house or wait for the possibility of getting a permanent visa to enter the United States. We finally decided to wait… and wait.

We were pretty much resigned to our fate of possibly remaining in Canada, when in 1960 John. F. Kennedy became President of the United States. Everything became accelerated. Not too long after, we received notice to go to the U.S. immigration office in Toronto for a health check-up and to fill out additional forms in preparation for our entry into the United States.

In the week we were to appear at the Toronto office, I learned that our fifteen-month-old daughter, Mariane, had been exposed to measles. She had a slight elevated temperature but had not yet developed a rash. Afraid that if we cancelled our appointment we might have another long wait, we decided to take a risk and go. When the U.S. Consulate doctor examined her, he remarked that she seemed awfully warm and I quickly explained that she had been asleep in my arms for at least an hour. He accepted that and we were given our permission to proceed.

We had to fill out numerous papers and answer hundreds of questions for each member of the family. What fascinated me most was that I had to even fill out the questionnaires for my three small children and since we were instructed to answer every question individually, I could not use "does not apply" as an answer. Imagine my amazement when I had to answer the questions for my baby daughter by writing a definite 'NO' to whether she was entering the United States for prostitution intentions or if she had ever been a prostitute. They wanted to know if she ever belonged to the Communist party or whether she or her young brother and sister had ever been charged with any felony offence. I kept printing a big NO after every question for all members of the family.

We returned to our home exhausted, but in our hands we finally held the magic papers that would allow us to come to America. We were jubilant!!! We were given four months to sell our house and contents. Our date of departure from Canada and entry into the United States would be June 10, 1961. It had been ten years since we had arrived in Canada and nothing would have kept us from meeting our deadline.

Our hearts were so elated with the realization of our final immigration to America that our immense workload in preparation could not put a damper on our endeavor. We sold our house at a very reasonable price, auctioned our furniture and other belongings and were ready to move by the scheduled date.

My brother Joe, who had also relocated to Canada, drove us to Dearborn, Michigan, a suburb of Detroit across from the Canadian border where relatives lived. We planned to spend a couple of days with my Uncle John and Aunt Tessie who had kindly vouched for our welfare as had been required by the Immigration and Nationalization Service. We crossed the border at Windsor, Ontario, with our final destination being California where the weather was similar to our homeland of Malta.

Our papers were all in order and our entrance into the United States went smoothly. The border personnel shook hands with us and were quite welcoming. My husband had designed and painted a poster with a big yellow sun and palm trees that read, "CALIFORNIA OR BUST" and had placed it in the back window of the car. As we drove slightly north to access the highway, a young man seeing our sign, yelled,

"Mister you're going the wrong way!"

We all had a good laugh. Our daughter Dianne still proudly displays this handmade poster in her home.

The two days at my uncle and aunt's house were spent celebrating and thanking them for their help and encouragement. As a token of our appreciation, we bought them a lovely gift, a tray table of walnut and glass on casters. On June 12th we boarded a plane to Los Angeles, California, at the Detroit airport. It was a new 707, considered huge at the time. A fellow passenger heard us discussing our plans and, acknowledging our excitement, gave each of our two older children a silver 50-cent piece. Their first American money! Our youngest was asleep in my arms, relaxed and content and quite unaware of the life-changing experiences that were taking place.

We were met in L.A. by Harry and Mary Bonnici, our long-time good friends and our son's godparents. They had preceded us from Malta to Canada and on to the U.S.A. several years before. We stayed with them for almost two weeks while we searched for an apartment and Tony looked for work. It was now time to face reality. We were finally in the country and state we most wanted to be in, but we had no job, no place of our own and savings of only $5,000. We had three young children and a lot of hope mixed with fear and questionable expectations.

Mary and Harry, who were doing well and owned their own home, in Rancho Palos Verdes, were in the midst of building a pool in their backyard. Waking up in the morning to watch the excavation and the plastering was like a good omen of things to come. We too were preparing a new foundation, a new beginning, and we were determined to see its fulfillment.

Since my husband did not want to work in a factory anymore, he began taking art classes by correspondence in preparation for a career change. When he had to draw nude women as part of his anatomy course, I found that I became very jealous. Likewise, Tony was ready to angrily confront any man who looked at me twice. We both seemed emotionally fragile and insecure.

I remember once, when we were still in Canada around Christmas time, we had gone shopping at Sears department store in Toronto, along with my brother Joe. It had been a treat for us to drive to the *big city* and I used to dress up for these special occasions, with hat, gloves and high heels. The store was very crowded with happy shoppers and at times, pushing through, I had to walk a few steps ahead of Tony. A man walking towards me smiled at me and said something under his breath. Tony leapt at him and would have punched him had not my brother held him back. The incident embarrassed me to no end. Yet had it been a woman who smiled at my husband and whispered some remarks, I would have burst into tears. I guess our insecurities showed themselves in very inappropriate behaviors.

Tony's first job in California was at Zody's, a discount retail store on Spring Street in Long Beach. He worked in a small cubicle making hand-painted display signs for the store. We found a cheap apartment on Western Avenue in San Pedro, not far from our Maltese friends Mary and Harry. We enrolled our children in school, bought a used car and began to settle down. Soon Tony complained that the small cubicle he worked in did not have good ventilation and paint vapors were giving him headaches. He found another job in Pasadena, north of Los Angeles, at a farmers' market called Prebles, where he again made hand-drawn signs, this time for the produce department.

We moved to Pasadena and rented a small house on Oxford Street. We were there to watch our very first live Rose Parade on January 1, 1962. We again tried to settle as best we could. We both started attending evening classes at Pasadena City College. Tony took a course in Commercial Art and I enrolled in my first Creative Writing class taught by Mrs. Richter. She was the wife of Professor Richter, the inventor of the seismological scale for measuring earthquakes, which was named after him.

Our life seemed to be going well. On weekends we'd drive to the shore at Santa Monica or Redondo Beach. The wonderful view of the Pacific Ocean always seemed to both excite and soothe us. We took a picnic basket and the children would love making castles in the sand. We even started looking at houses in a nice residential district of the Sierra Madre Hills area, and saved every penny we could towards purchasing a home of our own. Was our dream finally coming true?

But then one day Tony stunned me by confessing that he had been laid off from work for nearly two weeks. He cried and explained that every day he would get up in the morning and go to look for work. He had not told me before because he did not want to upset me. His instructor at the art class had encouraged him and had even given him a referral for a job interview. Tony never explained why he did not follow through and take advantage of this opportunity. He drove around for about four more days looking for work and finally found a job as a touch-up artist at the Buzza Cardoza greeting card company in Anaheim. We would have to move again.

Our children and I remained in our rented house in Pasadena while their dad drove to Anaheim to work and find an apartment for us. It saddened me when I learned that to save money, while searching for a place to rent, Tony had been sleeping in his car. One night he was awakened by the police because they thought he was a transient; how humiliating that must have been for him. In about two weeks we moved to an apartment on Philadelphia Avenue in Anaheim. We rented a truck and loaded our meager furniture along with a potted rubber tree that I had lovingly cared for. By the time we drove the 40 miles to Anaheim the wind had blown off every leaf from the plant and the lone main stem looked pitifully weak. It did not die, but as I looked at its poor condition I realized how much I could identify with it.

It was now 1963. We had moved three times in two years transferring the children from one school to the next. This was where we were living when we heard the tragic news that President John Kennedy had been shot.

That fateful day will always be as clear in my mind as if it happened yesterday. The apartment we lived in was in a complex where all the apartments' back doors opened into a large common backyard. We had no TV and I had been in the kitchen cooking when I heard a commotion outside. Residents of the other apartments were all gathering in the open yard with back doors left open and their TVs could be heard from outside. Curious, I opened my door and asked my neighbor,

"What is wrong? What has happened? Why is everyone so agitated?"

"Haven't you heard?" she asked with a quiver in her voice. "President Kennedy has been shot."

I stood there in disbelief and then slowly made my way to the next apartment where a crowd had gathered and the TV volume was turned up so everyone could hear. By now Kennedy had been rushed to the hospital. The news reports did not say that he had died, but that he had been gravely wounded. Mrs. Kennedy appeared stunned and confused, her suit covered with blood. I made my way back to our apartment, closed the door, fell into a chair and sobbed. This couldn't be happening to my President! To me, Kennedy was my hero. Not only because he happened to be the first Catholic President, but also because I believed his immigration policy had made it possible for my family to come to America.

My head ached and I just sat there unable to move or do anything. I do not know how long I had been sitting there when I heard the front door open and Tony walked in. He too had been crying and his first words were,

"They killed him."

I still don't understand whom he meant by 'they,' but I could see that he was very distraught. He lay on the bed and continued to cry, holding his head in both hands. We both felt at a loss for words.

During the next few days, watching the drama unfold on television was very heart breaking. We could not believe that this was really happening. A great sadness descended on me and my days seemed to pass in a trance. Tony went to work and the children attended school, but it was hard for us all to finally accept this tragic news.

Weeks passed and Tony had seemed happy in his work, but he had started complaining of pain in the left side of his face and a slight hearing loss in his left ear. His doctor gave him Vitamin B for his nerves and also diagnosed his symptoms as Tic Douloureux, pressure on the trigeminal nerve resulting in neuralgia. The pain can be excruciating and he had to take anti-convulsive medication. The doctor also prescribed Valium as he suspected the cause might be anxiety. The medications seemed to help and things went well for a while.

In 1929 my mother, Mary Georgio, was 19 years old and in love with my dad. She was quite fashionable, fluent in four languages, played tennis, and loved the opera.

At age 28 my father, John Serge, was courting my mother and working as a inspector for Malta's Health Department. He traveled extensively in Europe and was a radio aficionado.

Mother holding me at one year.

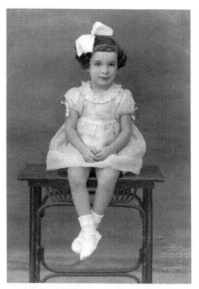

Formal posing at age three in my new
light blue voile dress...I loved that dress!

My First Holy Communion at seven years of age.

Me at 18 on the rooftop of my house.

Tony (standing top right) with his camping buddies.

Tony and I at the door to Sacro Cuor church on our wedding day.

Dad is escorting me down the aisle on my wedding day, March 10, 1951.

Tony and I beginning our dream life together.

Cutting our wedding cake.

Only a few days after our wedding, saying goodbye to Tony
as he leaves Malta to immigrate to Canada.

First photograph I received from Tony in Canada.
He's reading my letter and looking at my picture on the wall.

Me leaving Malta to join Tony in Canada; standing on left with my dad, sister Marlene, Aunt Evelyn, and brother Joe below.

The Greek steamer ship *Nea Hellas.*

I'm standing (second from left) with fellow passengers on the deck of the *Nea Hellas* sailing to Canada by way of New York.

My father at his office, as Superintendent of the Health Dept.
for the island of Malta.

The family I had left behind; Ronnie, Mum, Dad, Marlene and Joe.

In our Sunday best, ready for church.

Raising a family–Dianne, Jesse, baby Mariane, Me and Tony
on the back steps of our house in Canada.

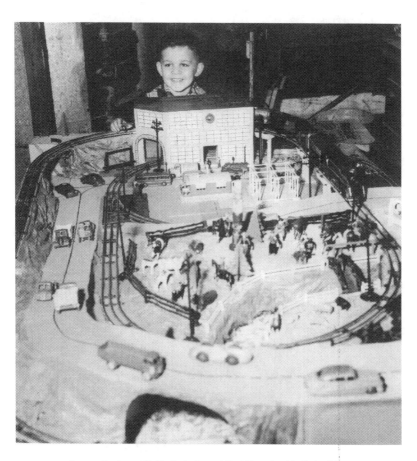

Jesse playing with his train layout that Tony had built for him.

Tony with trophy he won for his handmade ship model of the *Santa Maria*.

Tony in happier days building ship models.

Me and Tony in March, 1955.

I'm wearing a fancy taffeta dress that I sewed. I enjoyed sewing
and also made the curtains.

Tony in front of our house that was for sale in Oshawa, Canada.

This hand-painted sign was placed in the back window of the car
as we crossed the border into the United States.

Chapter Nine

A Diagnosis

Within three years of our arrival in California, we saved enough money to make a down payment on a house. Our three-bedroom home in Stanton had a huge backyard with fruit trees and a swing set for the kids. It was now March 1964 and we had finally put down roots. The children were enrolled in their new school and we spent the summer days picnicking at Huntington Beach State Park. All seemed to be going well again, or so I thought.

A few months after we moved into our new home the realtor who had sold us the house came by one day. He asked me how we were doing and if things were to our satisfaction. I thought that was awfully nice of him, but when Tony came home and I related the visit, he had a fit. He immediately phoned the realtor and warned him never to come to the house again during the day when he was not home.

By now I had grown accustomed to my husband's jealousy, but I began to worry about his seemingly overreaction to every simple thing. He complained that his facial pain and ringing in his ears had returned with increasing intensity. By the time we had been in our house for less than a year, it had gotten so bad that the slightest sharp noise would send him into a frenzy. When we had dinner the children had to be careful stirring their tea so the spoons would not clang against the side of the cups. Everyone was tense and worried. I tried to deny that anything was going wrong. I wanted so much to believe that my husband's pain was still only temporary, due to anxiety, and that the medications would eventually help him and we could fulfill our dreams.

In May of 1965, Tony turned 37 and to celebrate his birthday, his employer gave him a nice luncheon. Two months later we were invited to a Buzza Cardoza company pool party. I had never before been invited to a pool party at a place of business and I came face to face with cultural differences. I went dressed up in my best dress and high-heeled shoes while everyone else wore shorts, tee shirts and sandals. By the time I was introduced to Tony's boss my face had turned purple with embarrassment.

Tony's culture also conflicted with that of his coworkers. He was extremely insecure about being an immigrant and felt inferior to his workmates. In the fall, they would go hunting over the weekends. On Fridays they brought their hunting rifles to work, as they planned to leave straight from there and go to their hunting grounds. I recoiled in shock when Tony told me that he believed the guns were brought to the office as a personal threat to him. I tried to assure him that this was not the case, but he would not listen. He was suffering from a classic case of culture shock with overwhelming feelings of uncertainty and anxiety.

In an effort to become more Americanized, Tony decided to change our last name. He strongly felt that our Italian sounding name of 'Medati' had to be replaced with an English-sounding one. Discrimination was much more prevalent at that time. My daughter's friends, the Intravias, had had their house pelted with eggs. I went along with whatever he said. I had begun to notice the depth of his fears. Our whole family voted on a selection of different names and our name was legally changed to 'Marlin.'

Everything came to a head one morning when I received a phone call from Buzza Cardoza. As I clutched the phone to my ear, I heard the office manager's distressing news. He quietly and calmly informed me that my husband had lost his control and had threatened to jump out the window. They had notified the police and they had taken him to the mental ward at the Orange County Medical Center. My hands froze on the phone and I started to shake as I heard him say that Tony's employment had been terminated and that they would mail me his personal effects. I was instructed to go and meet my husband at the hospital.

I do not know what happened that made him want to jump out the window, other than he had felt threatened. Tony did not say anything and the police never talked to me, never asked me any questions. Later that day, he was released from the hospital into my care and I took him home. Being new in the United States we were very naive and very alone. We did not know where to get help. We had no family here and because we had moved from place to place we had no personal friends to lean on for guidance. Our old friends Mary and Harry Bonnici were supportive and always willing to listen, but they too were overwhelmed with our situation. Scared and lonely, I did not know what to do.

The following weeks were devastating. Tony insisted on going from doctor to doctor in a vain attempt of finding one who would agree with him that his medical problems resulted from the toxins in the paints he had been working with. He also insisted that I go with him. After each visit, the doctor would take me aside and tell me that my husband needed to have psychiatric help. I knew that Tony needed help, but I also knew that his pain was real. While he took his prescribed tranquilizers, his analgesics and his vitamins, I would still see him clutch his head in pain, gripping it tightly in both hands.

Our funds were dwindling. Tony applied for unemployment benefits, but because he had been fired he could not receive any compensation. However, because of the episode at work and his ongoing medical condition, he temporarily qualified for disability benefits. Soon he got the idea that he would get better treatment if he went to physicians in Beverly Hills instead of the county clinic. He believed that doctors did not care about poor immigrant people. He started going to different doctors in Los Angeles, paying $200 for each visit, yet with no better results.

Finally, one fateful day when he could not stand his head pressure anymore, I drove him to the Orange County Medical Center. This time x-rays and ultrasounds were ordered and the tests showed that he had an Acoustic Neuroma, a tumor behind his left ear. It affected his hearing and involved several facial nerves. He needed surgery as soon as possible.

My husband sat there stunned and it is hard to express how I felt. Initially I thought,

At last, a diagnosis. An identified medical sickness that can be treated.

However, as the doctor's statements penetrated my mind, I began to see our lives and dreams unraveling. The doctors explained the surgical process and discussed the dangers. They called the operation 'exploratory' as they were uncertain of the scope that the surgery required. One of the possibilities was that if it involved the spine, he could end up paralyzed in a wheelchair. Another was that he might have cancer. I could feel the blood drain from my head and go down to my feet.

I gripped the sides of the chair trying not to faint. My husband still looked as if he was in a trance. I cannot begin to imagine how he must have felt, though I think he began to show some relief at the thought that his throbbing head and ringing ears might eventually stop. I tried hard to stay focused on the solution and not think of all the bad things that could go wrong.

The preparation for surgery and the operation itself were scheduled within the next two weeks. My husband and I both returned home feeling very vulnerable, very scared and very confused. The following day while Tony rested in the early afternoon and our children were at school, I drove to St. Joseph's Hospital in Orange and requested to see a neurosurgeon. The hospital at that time was still run by Catholic nuns and seeing my nervous state and frightened look, one of the sisters escorted me to a waiting room. Being a Catholic I somehow felt more assured and less threatened at this hospital. I believed that a Catholic doctor would be more sympathetic to my family's crisis. A few minutes later a neurosurgeon entered the room and approached me. I blurted out my fears between shaking and sobbing and was taken aback when he started by asking me,

"What kind of medical insurance do you have?"

I explained that we were receiving disability benefits and were covered by the State Medical Assistance Program. He calmly informed me that he was well acquainted with the head of the Neurosurgery Department at the County hospital, Doctor Posnikoff, and he assured me that he had every confidence in him. I was then quietly led out of the room and out the door.

When I returned to my car I sat down in my seat and felt lost, bewildered and ignored. I had come here as a last-ditch of hope, maybe a consultation or an intervention. I don't know what I really expected but certainly not a question about my insurance. I drove home deciding to be strong no matter what. The children would soon be home from school and I did not want them to see me cry again.

The surgery was performed two weeks later at the Orange County Medical Center (now known as UCI Medical Center, part of the University of California at Irvine). I was highly nervous and afraid. I could not sit still and paced the waiting room floor feeling scared and numb. I began to pray as I had never prayed before. I had sent the kids to school and told them that I would pick them up after and bring them to see their father later in the day. I did not want them to witness my fear and instability. I went to use the restroom and was stunned to find a woman screaming and banging her head against the wall while relatives tried their best to calm her down. I soon learned that her 16-year-old son had been in a motorcycle accident and had not recovered from a deep coma. That brought my own fears into a better perspective. My situation seemed less distressing than hers. The waiting rooms and the bathrooms next to the surgery rooms were full of crying, scared and seemingly disconnected people who found themselves in desperate circumstances, some still hopeful and others in agony over a loss. How I wished my family could be with me and not be so far away.

A resident doctor, seeing me alone and noticing my stunned expression, offered to prescribe me a Valium. I had never had one before and I do not even know what dosage he gave me, but I had not eaten anything and it made me very sleepy. That actually made me angry. While I needed to relax I certainly did not want to go to sleep. The surgery took six hours and when I finally was allowed to see Tony I almost went into shock. His head and face were encased in bandages and his right eyelid and right side of his mouth drooped down. The surgeon explained that the operation required more extensive surgery than they had anticipated. They had to cut some nerves to remove the whole tumor that had affected his eye and his mouth and a second surgery would be needed in about a month to repair the nerve damage.

Later, as I left the room to let him rest and to go and pick up the kids from school, the woman visiting in the next bed touched my arm to comfort me and whispered,

"How is your father doing?"

I looked back in disbelief at my husband who was only three years older than me and realized how old he must look with his droopy face to people who did not know him.

We owned a very old Ford station wagon and on my way to the school it started to pour out smoke from the exhaust pipe. Soon I heard a police siren behind me and I eased to the curb to stop. By the time the officer came to my window I was a basket case. Tears rolled down my cheeks as I explained that I was on my way to get the children from school so they could visit their father who had just had an operation to remove a brain tumor.

"I do not know why the car is smoking," I sobbed, "I don't know what to do."

This was probably an experience the officer had never expected. He mumbled,

"I am sorry to hear that but please have the car fixed as soon as you can."

He put his pad back in his pocket and sent me on my way. It was a great relief and my gratitude must have shown.

I prepared the children for their visit with their father as best I could and explained his condition in brief. They were happy to see him, touched him and kissed him and did not voice any alarm over his appearance for which I was extremely grateful. I did not want them to worry about me so I hid my feelings. The next day when they left for school I again let the tears flow. I would pound the wall and cry out in desperation until I would fall exhausted, sobbing on the bed. Later I would get up, splash cold water on my face, put on some make-up to hide the dark circles under my eyes and drive to the hospital to be at my husband's side again.

I visited Tony every day in the hospital after the children left home for school. After about five days, while visiting, a nurse informed me that Dr. Prietto wanted to talk to me. He had been one of the resident surgical interns who had assisted during Tony's operation. He sat me down in a chair and asked me not to visit Tony every day.

"Why?" I asked, wondering what was wrong. He put his hand on mine and said,

"I can see you are very tired, anxious and on the verge of a breakdown."

It was true that my hands were shaking, but could he also tell that I had been crying myself to sleep every night and waking up every morning wondering how we were going to get through this? Tony had lost his job and we hardly had any savings left. He had just become disabled by the surgery and our future looked quite grim.

"He expects me to visit him," I stammered. He smiled and said,

"I will tell him it's doctor's orders, that it is for his benefit." I nodded, not knowing what to say. I did need a rest. Dr. Prietto went on,

"Go to the beach tomorrow, take a long walk." Then he asked me,

"How are you managing financially? Are you able to pay your mortgage?"

I confessed that we were using our meager savings and that the money will soon run out, that we were new in this country, we had no family and that I did not know where to go for advice. He replied,

"Homestead your house, an attorney can do that for you and it will protect you against creditors."

He then referred me to Social Services for welfare aid. Dr. Prietto went beyond his medical profession and provided me with a light at the end of the tunnel. I am forever grateful.

Tony's second surgery was performed a month later. They took a nerve from behind his tongue and placed it in his cheek to replace the one they had to cut. It lifted his drooping face but pulled it to one side when he smiled. Still it was an improvement. Soon however, other problems started to surface. The numbness in Tony's right cheek never got better and he could not blink well, consequently he needed to use eye drops frequently to prevent his eye from drying out.

As the weeks went by, Tony started to feel very discouraged. His doctors decided to fit him with a clear plastic eye cover in the hope that it would keep his eye better lubricated. It looked like a contact lens and covered his whole eye but it proved to be very uncomfortable. His eye eventually became infected and the artificial lens had to be removed.

Tony also had to relearn to write, as his right hand was shaky and weak from the surgery. He was given electric stimulation to his lower arms to rejuvenate some of the nerves that had been affected. I did not understand why his hands and arms were not fully functional, but I guess it is like when one suffers a stroke; his brain tumor surgery had impaired his nerve connections.

Weeks turned into months and he slowly started to physically improve. By now, we were on Welfare and both my husband and I found this situation to be very degrading. I reluctantly realized that this was a necessity for the time being, but my husband couldn't cope with being unable to take financial care of his family. It was contrary to our culture and our American Dream. Psychologically he took a downward turn.

At this dreadful time my husband and I had been married for 14 years, and I had the nagging fear that the children were losing their father, as his psychological condition was not good and his anger escalated. Though I tried to reassure myself that they were too young to fully comprehend the depth of the crisis we were in, nonetheless, I knew that they could feel and see the tension and the anxiety we were experiencing. I yearned to have someone to pour my heart out to and I did not want my parents to know all about our problems or share with them our dire situation. They had not wanted me to marry Tony and I did not want to hear "I told you so," although surely nobody can predict when or if an illness will strike. Before his sickness, Tony had been a hard worker and was a good father and husband aside from his jealousies and insecurities. My brother Joe was now married and still lived in Canada. It was with him that I shared most of my concerns and fears. His willingness to bear the brunt of my venting was a consolation I am ever thankful for.

Chapter Ten

Getting Help

My first contact with the Welfare Department occurred in 1965 when a social worker at the Orange County Medical Center handed me some forms to fill out. I was instructed to write down our source of income, place of residence, monthly mortgage, car payments, utility bills, loans and other outstanding payments along with food expenses. They also wanted to know how much money we had in the bank, if any, and even any amount of cash on hand. I recall that I had opened my purse and actually counted all the paper bills, silver quarters, dimes and even the pennies! This was all new to me and I was determined to fill out everything right! There were a lot of pages, but I did not mind; I was actually relieved that someone cared and that assistance was available. My husband had been the sole financial support of our family, as he had not wanted me to work. He sincerely felt that a mother should be home raising the children and tending to the family needs. I had no qualms about that because I too fervently believed that my place was at home, cooking healthy meals and keeping house.

Unless you have ever had to apply for welfare help or had been completely unaware of such insurance as I had been, it may be hard to understand what a life saving support this program was. It wasn't much money, but at least I could buy some food and have help towards the house payment while we tried to figure out some way to get back on our feet. Our needs were few. Coming from a different culture, my husband and I did not believe in using credit for our purchases. We either could afford to buy something or we did without, so other than the house payment, utilities and food, we had no other monthly debts.

I felt very fortunate about this until I came across what I perceived to be an injustice. Our thriftiness and modest living had seemingly backfired. We had an old TV, an old used transportation car, a secondhand stove and refrigerator and I hung the wash on the line to dry. We had saved up and paid cash for these so when our welfare support payments were calculated we had nothing to deduct. Had we purchased a new car, a TV, a new washer and dryer and kitchen appliances on credit we would have been making monthly installments, and we would have received a larger allotment. Of course I would not want to see a family who had a similar unfortunate experience lose their possessions because they could not make the payments, but as it happened, because we had been reluctant to buy on credit and had sacrificed to live only on what my husband earned, ultimately we seemed to have been indirectly penalized. Had we indulged in credit buying, it would have been to our own benefit.

We received welfare support for several months while I tried to plan what I needed to do. The social worker advised me to stay home and continue to take care of the family as I had been doing. She felt that they needed me home to ease the trauma. I was sure there was truth in this, but I also knew that if we remained on welfare it would become increasingly difficult to rebound financially. I began taking in ironing to help towards our support and also started looking for work. I had never held a job outside the home and only had a high school education at the time so my choice of employment was very limited. I was still young though, only 34 years old, and willing to try anything.

Tony insisted on coming with me in the car when I went job hunting. We loaded the kids in the back seat of our '59 station wagon and off we went. Since I had no idea where to start looking, I drove to an industrial area not too far from our house. To my delight one of the manufacturers, a beverage bottling company, had a sign posted for "HELP WANTED." I parked and ventured inside while my husband and our kids anxiously waited in the car. The woman who was doing the hiring explained to me that the job required good dexterity. I would have to replace filled bottles with empty ones when they passed by me on a conveyer belt. I confessed that I had never worked in a factory before, but I had three children to feed and a sick husband and was willing to work very hard.

I do not know if she took pity on me or was in extreme need of workers, but she took me into another room where a mock-up of a work area had been installed. Empty pop bottles in containers were placed by my side and filled bottles started moving on a circular belt in front of me. She instructed me to replace each one as they went by, switching the filled bottle from the conveyer with the empty one from the container at my side. As I began the process she started a stopwatch. I eagerly did what I was asked to do even though I had never done such menial work before, yet I felt sad at the realization that our dream of coming to America had come to this. My children and my husband were all depending on me now. I must not fail. She timed me for about ten minutes and then told me that I should come on the next day, Friday, for a physical and that I should be able to start work on Monday. The pay was close to minimal wage, but it would take us off welfare, and that had been our goal.

I thanked her and practically flew out the door to go and tell my family the good news. The children clapped for joy, but Tony said nothing. As I drove back home he finally said,

"You might as well call that employer and tell her that you are not taking the job."

"Why?" I gasped. I felt light headed and confused. It seemed as if I had been twirling in a merry-go-round that was never going to stop.

"No wife of mine," Tony said, "is going to take factory job."

So why had he agreed to let me even try? Was he hoping I'd fail? He believed that without his support I could not survive and he had wanted to prove it. His manhood was at stake. Yet I had gotten the job at my first try, even without any experience. With this episode, I began to understand that if he did not get well, I was going to have to start making my own decisions. But for now, I cancelled the employment.

At my begging and insistence, my social worker informed me of a new Government Program called M.D.T.A. (Manpower Development and Training Act) where the Employment Department was giving aptitude tests and interviewing for a much needed Nursing Program. I had to qualify as 'Head of Household,' which I did since my husband claimed disability.

I easily passed the aptitude test, but then the employment office recruiter called me with the disappointing news that the Nursing

Program already had 300 applicants for only 28 openings at the local college selected for this assignment.

"Make me number 301," I begged.

I had always considered nursing a choice profession and I was desperate for this opportunity. I insisted on being included as one of the applicants and even though my chances were slim, I was allowed to apply.

After more questions and tests, I later received a phone call informing me that I had been chosen as one of the fortunate few selected to attend Orange Coast College in Costa Mesa for the two-year Licensed Vocational Nursing Program. I literally jumped for joy! The Government would pay for my books and I would receive a transportation allowance. This new program would replace the welfare payments that we had been receiving. We were to sustain ourselves on $68 a week. It would be worth the sacrifice.

Chapter Eleven

Education and Training

I entered the Nursing program with great enthusiasm. This being my first experience at an American college campus, I was enthralled. With a 35-minute drive, I had to leave home before the children got ready for school. I prepared their school lunches the night before and thanked God that they never complained. I felt safe in the knowledge that although their father was not well enough to go to work, he could still get up in the morning and help them if needed and he would be home when they returned from school. Looking back I am still amazed how, even in these critical times, our children managed to continue getting excellent grades in their school reports. By this time their ages were 13, 11 and 6 years old. They were all attending St. Polycarp Catholic School in Garden Grove and my dear neighbors helped in their transportation to and from the school grounds.

On the way home from my classes, I usually stopped at McDonald's to pick up something for dinner. We sustained ourselves on hamburgers and French fries for months on end. I never arrived home before five in the evening and after the kids did their homework, watched a little TV and then prepared for bed, I started my studies that often times dragged into the night. Our house was small; we ate in the kitchen as we had no separate dining room. Neither did we have an office or study room, so after the children went to bed was the only time I could use the kitchen table as my desk and also have the quiet I needed to concentrate on my homework.

At this time our son Jesse was in the 8th grade and had a very encouraging schoolteacher. Mr. Southern knew what Jesse was going through and admired his drive to become class President in spite of the turmoil at home. Furthermore he motivated Jesse to participate in the play *Our Town* in the role of Dr. Gibbs.

Tony and I had originally planned to enroll Jesse at Servite, a private Catholic college preparatory high school in Anaheim; however, we were now unable to afford the class tuition. By the end of the school year we were notified that an anonymous donor had paid Jesse's tuition for his first year at Servite. To this day, I strongly believe that his benefactor was none other than Mr. Robert Southern.

Jesse continued at Servite by skipping his lunch periods to work in the cafeteria in lieu of paying tuition. He also helped his teachers after school until he was able to get a part-time job and pay for his schooling. He made us all proud when he graduated. He then attended C.S.U. in Fullerton where he earned a B.S. degree in biology while working full-time at an Alpha Beta supermarket. Later he received an M.B.A. from Pepperdine University in Malibu, California. He is now a Clinical Research Management Consultant dealing with new medical devices and advising on federal approval requirements. If it was Mr. Southern, his influence and support have certainly been a pivotal point in my son's studies and achievements.

We were very poor the first Christmas after Tony had his surgery and before I started my nursing classes, but our good neighbors rallied to our support. Gloria, who lived five houses down from ours, was a volunteer for our church's program to help the needy. She asked us what we needed and suggested that each child list five items so the donors can have a variety to pick one from. Our gift lists included such things as slippers, pajamas, toilet items, school clothes and a few personal items. Imagine our surprise when the doorbell rang on Christmas Eve and our neighbors brought in boxes filled with all the five presents for each child plus a turkey with all the fixings.

The kids joyfully laid out their gifts side by side around our aluminum Christmas tree and were ecstatic to see that they covered most of the living room floor. They had never had this many Christmas presents and all were so beautifully wrapped in colored foil. Dianne was overjoyed to have received both the coveted pink crystal rosary beads and a blue birthstone ring that she had included in her list! Jesse and Mariane were also both thrilled with the gifts they received which made our Christmas much happier than we had anticipated. Reading the signed Christmas card, I realized that this was much more than a church donation. In fact all my neighbors had contributed and shopped for all the items we listed. Their love and support was overwhelming to me and to my children, but unfortunately for my husband, it further emphasized his inability to provide for us. He only seemed to look at the negative aspects of our condition and nothing anybody said or did helped to relieve his depression.

I encouraged Tony to start looking for a job. I strongly believed that contributing to the family income would be the only way for him to regain his self-worth and dignity. He had been working to improve his hand coordination, practicing his writing and slowly overcoming his shakiness that had resulted from his surgeries. It was an arduous process that had begun with a game-like step when he would 'sign-in' at the dinner table before each meal. After many months of home therapy including electrical stimulation, he had greatly strengthened his muscles, yet I could not help feeling totally stunned when one day he told me that he had been hired by a local drafting firm. My happiness overflowed. I was ashamed to admit to myself that my hopes that this would actually happen had been very slim.

While I was in the nursing program, every Monday I had to fill out a state form declaring that I was still the head of the household for the family. The following Monday, I proudly answered this question again and wrote, "Husband started working this week." I was honest and too naive to comprehend the full impact of that happy acknowledgement. What a mistake it turned out to be. Everything crashed around me. A few days later a letter arrived from Sacramento informing me that since my husband was now employed and thus recognized as the head of the household, I no longer qualified for enrollment and was therefore being dropped from the State Funded Nursing Program. I could hardly believe it. I had thought that things were beginning to improve. I had studied hard and was getting A's on my assignments, but again everything seemed to be slipping away. I was midway through my nursing program, my gateway to a profession that would help me earn a living, yet was being terminated because I had encouraged my husband to seek work. I was heartsick. I felt lost and bewildered. I saw myself losing everything I had strived so hard for.

Amid my confusion, however, I felt a spark of hope at the prospect that Tony might regain his health completely and be the breadwinner again as he so much wanted and needed to be. But a few days later he was discharged from work. The strain of a full day's work had proved to be too much for him. He evidently had not yet been ready for the responsibility of this position. The knowledge that he had tried and failed and the fact that it had negatively affected my nursing program sent him spinning into an emotional breakdown. He ended up in the Crisis Ward of the Orange County Medical Center. The doctors examined him, prescribed stronger drugs for depression and anxiety, and again released him back home into my care.

Tony continued to mistrust his doctors, suspecting that they were telling him one thing while writing conflicting information in his chart. One day he went to the hospital, walked into a doctor's lounge and slipped into a white tunic that was hanging on a coat rack. He then went down to the filing office and, claiming to be a visiting doctor, requested his own chart. He signed for the papers with a fictitious name and left. Seems unbelievable, but it really happened. How amazing that he could be so creative and so clever yet be so determined to prove that he had been poisoned. He remained reluctant to accept his tumor diagnosis and move on. He took his chart to a Xerox machine, returned the original, brought the copies home and no one was the wiser.

He did not find anything in the medical notes that would justify his suspicions of poisoning. He did read that the doctors had noted that he could possibly be suffering from schizophrenia. This made him angry and even more determined to prove them wrong.

The following weeks were a constant turmoil for me. Writing letters of explanation to Sacramento, calling and visiting the Santa Ana employment office that had enrolled me in the nursing program and having instructors at Orange Coast College plead my case. Finally, to my great relief, I was readmitted to the classes. This turned out to be the last nursing class under the M.D.T.A. State Program. That year, Governor Brown who had initiated the program, was defeated and the newly elected Governor Reagan, cancelled its support. On the day of graduation, all the graduates received a card from the State of

California, thanking us for finishing the program and congratulating our achievement. To my dismay, the card had a photo of Governor Reagan pasted over one of former Governor Brown.

During our nursing training, my class of 28 students was assigned to different hospitals to earn experience in various departments. We worked in Cardiac Units, Cancer Wards, Pediatrics, Burn Units, Surgery and Intensive Care. We were usually given one patient each to care for under the supervision of a staff nurse. We started at the 7 a.m. morning shift until lunchtime after which we would return to the college for lectures, exams, reports and assignments for the following day. Each of these specialized hospital training sessions lasted six weeks.

Things at home were not getting any better. Tony would study books from the library dealing with industrial poisons and toxic environments and confront me as soon as I got home with a list of far-fetched reasons why he believed he had been poisoned. He began to suspect that he had been operated on, not to remove a brain tumor, but to scare him and prevent him from going on with his investigations into work-related abuses of pollutants. I did not doubt that maybe working with paints and inks in poorly ventilated rooms may have contributed to his illness, but I could not go so far as to believe that the doctors had lied about him having a tumor. He also vehemently believed that a popular TV show, *The F.B.I.* starring Efrem Zimbalist Jr., had specific messages and warnings for him. This was inconceivable to me, but Tony would get very upset and angry if I disagreed about anything he said.

The strain of these day-to-day, week-to-week, fluctuating emotions was beginning to take a heavy toll on me. It was December of 1966 and Christmas was fast approaching again. My study group had been assigned to a hospital in South Laguna Beach. During this time of year the early morning fog rolled in across Pacific Coast Highway from the ocean. I would leave the house at 5:30 a.m. while it was still dark to allow me enough leeway, because by the time I reached Huntington Beach the thick fog would almost obscure the taillights of the cars ahead of me. With no visible bearings I would be completely lost and would drive at a slow crawl along this winding road. At this early hour the sun had not yet penetrated the soupy atmosphere and I was never quite sure whether I was following the curve of the road or close to driving off the cliff.

One particularly bad morning, I was overcome with dread and felt that my life had started down on an unending spiral. I could no longer see my way out of my personal storm. I had dealt with Tony's surgery and long illness and our resulting poverty, but these last years of unrelieved tension with no end in sight had me confused, disillusioned and fatigued. My mind was as hazy as the fog on P.C.H. I could not see where the road turned and neither could I see how to put an end to my pain. It seemed to me as if all my efforts were to no avail. A terrible thought entered my mind,

Drive off the cliff and it will be all over… step on the gas and end it.

Suddenly my thoughts turned back to my three children. *What would they do? How would they cope and survive? What message would I be leaving them?*

Tears filled my eyes and blocked my view even more. I wanted to stop the car but feared that vehicles behind me would slam into mine. I realized that I did not really want to die; I just wanted this pain, this steady ache in my heart to go away. As I reached South Laguna, the rising sun had begun to filter through a few areas and I could finally identify a number of landmarks. Arriving at the hospital I sensed a great relief at the dawn of another day.

Our assignment at the Laguna hospital was hard and strenuous. We were dealing with patients who had had prostate or bladder surgeries. Some of these patients were elderly and obese and it was a struggle to help them out of bed and into a wheelchair. In really difficult cases two or more nurses were required, but mostly we were on our own. The patients did their very best to help, but we also had to contend with urine bags, tubes, surgical dressings and I.V. fluids hanging on poles. Often we had to change the bed linen with the patient still in the bed, turning them to one side and then the other while slipping the sheets under them. By the end of the shift I would be exhausted and began to wonder how nurses who had six or more patients managed to survive. Eventually, we also tended cardiac and orthopedic patients that proved equally challenging. After six weeks in each of the surgery departments, around the end of January 1967, we were again assigned to the Orange County Medical Center, this time to the Psychiatric Ward.

Our assignments were chosen to coincide with our class lessons. In the Psychiatric Ward everyone was ambulatory now and our patients were on medication and receiving counseling. We had been instructed to mingle and chat, observe and learn, but no matter how outrageous their stories were, we should only listen and sympathize but make no comment nor give any advice.

At age 39 my husband should have been in the prime of his life. Instead, he was at home unemployed, on medication and unable to cope with his reality. He felt overwhelmed and was angry at the world. His eye continued to give him problems, needing frequent care because he still could not blink due to his facial paralysis. Recovery was very slow. He started typing letters to various organizations asking them to investigate his doctors, suggesting that he had not had a brain tumor but was sick from toxic poisoning. He even wrote that the F.B.I. had been aware of this and were in cahoots with the doctors. He wrote to the Medical Commission that investigates complaints against doctors and to the Knights of Columbus in Chicago, of which he was a member. He wrote to our Congressman and to the Maltese Consulate in Los Angeles. Some of these people responded by sending him forms to fill out and return, which he immediately took as a denial for help, since he had expected them to take his word and arrest the doctors. Each day he seemed to grow more agitated and finally, at the insistence of our social worker, his doctors were somehow able to convince him to willingly enter the hospital's psychiatric ward as an in-patient. They explained to him that this way they could monitor his responses to the medications and adjust the dosages as needed to improve his health and well-being.

I had not confided this turn of events to my instructors at the nursing school, afraid it may jeopardize my assignment. Visiting the Psychiatric Ward as a student and now also seeing my husband there as a patient, was very painful and hard to handle. Concealing my sadness and my nervousness seemed to be almost impossible. One day Tony approached me, proudly showing me an ashtray he had made out of miniature tiles in a craft therapy class. He looked so pathetic, so small, like a little boy showing his mother his new toy. I then realized that the doctors and the therapists were treating him as a physically brain damaged individual and that he seemed more heavily sedated than before. The doctors never consulted with me regarding the medications they were giving him.

I finally had to approach my instructors and explain my situation; that seeing him daily like this was interfering with my ability to function. They were very understanding and transferred me to a different floor were other students were also participating.

After seeing my husband in this deteriorated state, I requested a meeting with his doctors. I told them how concerned I was about his condition, that he seemed overly medicated and that I could not see any improvement. They said they would look into it. However, two weeks later they informed me that they were again releasing him to come home in my care. He was on Mellaril, Valium, and Vitamin B. He had to continue the electrical stimulation to his arms and hands and also instill lubricating drops in his eye on a regular basis. At times I felt that if I had been in his situation, I too might have given up, stayed in denial and tried to prove that outside forces were the cause of my situation. Who can tell how each one of us would react under such unpredictable and unending stress.

In January of 1967 I became a citizen of the United States of America while at this sad stage in my life. Citizenship was a requirement to get my Nursing License, but becoming an American had always been my life-long dream. I was among a large number of people who received our citizen papers at the Santa Ana Court House in Orange County and our photo appeared in the Orange County Register. This was a meaningful milestone of which I am very proud and grateful. Tony was too sick at the time to apply for citizenship and so the children had to pursue citizenship independently after they each turned eighteen.

By the summer of the same year, I was close to the end of my nursing program. My class had concluded our studies, read all our textbooks and completed testing. All of us were agog with anticipation. We had been together every day for two years and wanted a reminder of our time together. We decided to each contribute a poem or an essay about our experiences and have it printed in a souvenir booklet. We took photos, drew caricatures of our instructors and added remarks, some serious and some funny, about things that happened during the times we all shared together. We also described our frustrations:

Misery is:

- *Not being able to make rounded square corners (bed sheets).*
- *A cold bedpan.*
- *Dressing in gown, mask, cap and gloves for isolation treatment of patients and realizing that you left needed equipment outside the room.*
- *Taking a ten-minute break and on returning the charge nurse tells you that you could have taken fifteen.*
- *Getting up early to get to school and your car won't start.*
- *Getting to class at 8 o'clock sharp and not finding any of your classmates on campus and you left your schedule notebook at home.*
- *Going to the wrong hospital on the first day of a new assignment.*

At some time or another we all seemed to have shared these moments. We also had grateful memories:

- *Seeing a sick patient go home in good health.*
- *A scrub dress that fits.*
- *Hearing a doctor say "Thank you" to you.*
- *Hearing our instructor call "class adjourned."*
- *Good results from an enema.*
- *Knowing that your nursing care has improved the patient's condition.*
- *Graduation Day, when at long last you have reached the end of that rainbow that had seemed so far away.*

We had begun to wonder about our future employment. During our last six weeks of training, we had the option to work at the hospital and the department of our choice, and thus gain more experience in a particular field of interest. As my selection I picked Pediatrics and was assigned to Children's Hospital of Orange County (C.H.O.C.). I chose Pediatrics because in my various previous assignments, I had felt really close to the helpless little ones and also had a very good rapport with their mothers. Being a mother myself, I could easily empathize with their concerns and anxieties.

Before this assignment was completed, the head nurse, Mrs. Myers, asked me if I would like to work there. I was overjoyed. I had not even completed the program and I already had a job offer. Only one obstacle remained. To receive my nursing license I had to pass the two-day State Board exams being held in Santa Monica in September.

The College sponsored our graduation dinner party at the Revere House in Santa Ana and our families were invited. It was a monumental celebration for us who had struggled the past two years to reach this goal. The instructors presented us with our diplomas at the end of the dinner and most of us had tears in our eyes as we bid them and each other goodbye and offered our best wishes. I easily passed the State Board exam and started work at Children's Hospital in September of 1967. It was the beginning of my nursing career that would last 18 years.

Chapter Twelve

Career Start

Working at Children's Hospital gave me a boost both emotionally and financially. We now were able to get off welfare and my husband was still collecting his disability benefits. Sixteen-year-old Jesse was now a junior at Servite high school in Anaheim. Dianne, fourteen, was starting Rosary high school in Fullerton and Mariane, eight, was still enrolled at St. Polycarp elementary in Garden Grove. Their transportation to each school was now accomplished with different car pools. I helped drive to St. Polycarp on my days off from work. Tuition was a bit high and even with me working full-time we could barely make ends meet, but a good education would ensure the children's better future so we sacrificed to send them to these private Catholic schools.

Nursing has its rewarding and also sad moments. I loved taking care of the children and comforting their parents, but it wasn't easy seeing them suffering with leukemia, cystic fibrosis, heart disease or other life-endangering ailments. When a child died it would take me a long time to accept it. I had to learn that these things happen and eventually began to feel thankful that, in some small way, I had been able to contribute to their care and their parents' solace. The children that really affected me were the burn patients. I had to daily place them in a bath under sterile conditions and, after medicating them, I had to scrub off their dead skin. It was torture for them as well as for me. Even with medication they could still feel pain and my heart ached for them.

One of my most interesting patients was a two-year-old girl from Vietnam. It was during the Vietnam War and one of our hospital doctors, who had been stationed there, learned about this young child with a heart defect. She needed surgery to survive so doctors at C.H.O.C. gave their services free of charge. An airline donated transportation for the girl and her mother and they became quite the media event. The little patient, who we called Suzie, proved to be quite a challenge. She had suffered from malnutrition and her lips and fingernails were blue because of poor circulation as a result of her frail heart condition.

The doctors cut through her sternum and mended her heart, but because of her initial poor condition her incision took a long time to close and heal. To offset the possibility of infection the doctors ordered all nurses responsible for her care to wear masks, gowns, caps and sterile gloves. We cleaned and disinfected her incision daily. Most amazing was that I could see inside her chest through the open wound and observe her beating heart. It was an experience I will never forget. Eventually her incision healed and closed and after four months she and her mother were able to return to Vietnam.

Being busy and absorbed with the tasks I had to perform at work often helped me to forget my own problems at home; however, as soon as I entered the door to my house I felt swamped again with the ever-present turmoil. My husband still bombarded me and launched into his daily litany of quotes from medical books, trying to convince me that his doctors lied and his suffering had resulted from unhealthy work conditions. It took all my physical and emotional strength to listen to him, prepare dinner and oversee the children doing their homework. After they were in bed, my husband insisted that I read what he had noted in the books. I gently agreed or disagreed with what he showed me trying hard not to upset him. When I returned to work, my fellow nurses would be talking about their past weekends, their ski trips, their visit to some exotic place or their family gatherings, but all I sadly had to talk about was my husband's latest delusions so I kept my mouth shut.

By mid-spring of 1969 I was feeling exhausted. I needed a break or I was not going to be able to continue functioning under these constant and stressful conditions. In May, Dianne wrote me this pick-me-up note:

Dear Mom,

First I would like to tell you a very important thing. "HAPPY MOTHER'S DAY." You thought I forgot didn't you? Well, I didn't. Aren't you proud of me? You know mom, I'm a teenager now, believe it or not, but my feelings toward you are still the same as when I was your little "Nincompoop." I know I see you every day, but I thought a note would be nice.

Dianne.

She made my day! 'Nincompoop' was a pet name I had used when she was little.

My mother then offered to pay part of my passage to go for a holiday in Malta. It had been 18 years since I had left the island and my father's health had deteriorated. Anxious to see my family again, I decided to accept her offer. That summer I went with daughter Mariane, now nine, for a two-week visit back to my home country. Jesse and Dianne were then 17 and 15-years-old and quite mature enough to remain home with their father. In fact, I was pleased to later learn that Dianne had done most of the cooking and laundry and Jesse had helped his father to complete a major house project.

Chapter Thirteen

My Visit Home

Returning to Malta after so many years filled me with wonder. I had left by ship and was returning by plane, which offered me a first-time aerial view of my dear island home. The contrast was stunning. I had left my stucco and wood home in California and now looked down on a solid bleached rock with houses made of large stone blocks. The stones are left in their natural light color so, as I looked down from the plane, the buildings were reflecting the bright sun back to me. Although the island has many tropical plants, flowers and palm trees, there are not many large foliage trees and no green lawns.

My mother and brother came to meet Mariane and me at the airport. I then learned that my father was in a wheelchair and too ill to come and join us. My brother Ronnie was now married and had five children. He came in his own car. I was glad to see that the island had regained its pre-war standards and the people seemed to be doing well. My mother, of course, was older, but her physical appearance had not changed much. The next day I met my brother's lovely wife Rose for the first time and their youngest baby John who had been born only a few weeks before our arrival. My sister Marlene who was 11-years-old when I left Malta was now a young woman of 29 years. She came to Malta for a holiday a few days before we had to leave. She had moved to Canada in 1967 and lived close to my brother Joe. Up to that time she had still lived at home and was a great help to mum and dad, as was the custom for unmarried ladies at the time. We managed to spend the last week together before we both had to return to our new homeland.

Going back home is never the same as when you left it. Malta was an independent country now with a booming dockyard business servicing and repairing international ships in the Grand Harbour. Tourism had become its biggest livelihood. Tourists were eager to fill the new and rebuilt hotels and purchase the world-renowned handmade lace and hand-blown glass. Other tourists came to study Malta's prehistoric ruins and to visit the area where St. Paul is said to have been shipwrecked before being taken to Rome, where he was beheaded. He is credited with converting the island to Christianity.

Germans and Italians who had practically destroyed the island with bombs were now swimming in the clear inviting blue sea. It is ideal for scuba divers who come from all over the world to enjoy and explore the beautiful Mediterranean Sea. Ferries take you for day trips around the island and water skiers and sunbathers abound.

My father, besides being confined to a wheelchair, appeared very ill. He was pale and had lost a lot of weight, but his eyes lit up and he shook with excitement as he realized that his 'little girl' was back home and had brought him a granddaughter to meet him for the first time. It was so wonderful to see him and yet so sad to find him in that condition. I had memories of my father as a vibrant man with his voice bouncing off the walls as he belted out arias from his favorite operas while mother played the piano. Now he could not even walk.

We slept at my parents' house and during the day we visited relatives and old friends and enjoyed restaurants that were now being patronized by a new generation. Some of them had been rebuilt, but many of them were brand new and very modern. The island was humming, especially in the evenings with theaters and international club shows, discos and jazz festivals. It would be late at night when we returned to my parents' house. I recall how I resented that my father would get out of bed and ease himself into his wheelchair so that he could come to see if my daughter and I were all right and safely home.

My goodness, I would say to myself, *I am a grown woman, the mother of three children who has traveled thousands of miles on my own to come here to visit. Surely I do not need to be checked on when I came home. Did I have to be treated like a little kid?*

Of course now I realize that that was exactly what I seemed to him. His little girl had returned home and his heart was so full of love, he wanted to make sure that no harm had come to his precious daughter and granddaughter while they were under his care. Also, in his weakened condition, he may have just wanted to make sure that we were really there and it wasn't just a dream!

My father passed away the following year. It is too late now to tell him how sorry I am for being so inconsiderate and not understanding that behind his actions, which I resented at the time, had lingered the great love that he felt for us mingled with the knowledge that we would soon be leaving again. He had to safely guard these moments that were so precious to him. I could not see it then, but forty years have passed since and now my own children have grown and left my home and when they visit I often say,

"Be careful. Take care. Are you hungry? Are you cold? Wear a sweater. Are you hot? Drive carefully."

One's children are always one's children no matter how old they get and the cycle continues.

Some changes on the island included the new Hilton, Ramada and Radisson Resort Hotels and many new and refurbished local ones as well. Also McDonalds, Pizza Hut, Winchell's Donuts and Burger King were now thriving businesses there. The dockyards were always kept busy repairing and maintaining the stream of foreign yachts that filled the harbor and marinas. Many locals now owned cars, but the old narrow streets were originally built for horses and motorbikes so navigation by auto was not easy and there was a constant blowing of horns. There are still very few traffic lights. The Maltese drive on the left side of the street as they do in Britain and they drive *fast*. An old joke in Malta says that you do not drive to the left or to the right… you try to drive in the shade!

Everyone in Malta speaks both Maltese and English so I refrained from speaking Maltese so that Mariane would not feel left out of the conversation. Tony and I had not taught our children to speak Maltese, as we wanted them to assimilate early and be able to speak English before they entered school. Two of my brother's daughters were close to my daughter in age and could speak English so she got on well with her newfound cousins.

It was 'Festa' time while we were there. These summertime religious fiestas were being celebrated throughout the island, with each village celebrating its patron saint. They all compete with decorations, fireworks, parades and local bands. The one in my hometown of Sliema takes place on the first Sunday of July so we were there to witness the colorful street decorations and all the celebrations. The outside of our church was all lit up with hundreds of white sparkling bulbs and the life-size statue of the Madonna holding the child Jesus was presented to the cheering crowds on an adorned wooden platform supported on the shoulders of eight strong men. This procession left the church with the ringing of bells and harmonious singing and was paraded down one street and up another ending back at the church some three hours later to the welcoming booms of loud fireworks and the church club marching band. Young boys and priests led the parade carrying lighted candles and young girls threw flower petals in front of the statue from hand-held baskets. To the local parishioners and tourists alike, this is a very emotional spectacle.

Some people walked behind the statue following the procession while others lined the streets or went to their second-story balconies or rooftops, where they cheered and showered the statue with confetti as it passed by. I remember how as a child I used to collect the silver paper lining from discarded cigarette boxes. Since my uncles were heavy smokers, it did not take me long to collect a shoebox full. My friends and I would plan for this special event well in advance. We would shred the silver paper by hand and then throw it from the balcony as the beautiful statue of Our Lady came down the street past our house.

It's a festivity that the locals still look forward to and prepare for all year long. Tourists continue to time their vacation visits around these celebrations. The ceremonies usually last three whole days and are followed by others in different villages. There is always a great fireworks display at the end of each fiesta. It's an impressive experience to remember no matter what your religious preference might be.

This June of 1969 had been most memorable being also the month and year that Americans landed on the moon. I could not have felt more proud to be an American on that fateful day. At that time there were only three TV stations on Malta and the TV report covering this historical event was being transmitted from Italy, the closest land. It was hard to disguise my disappointment at being able to only watch a delayed broadcast of the moon landing in Italian, when I wanted so much to see it as it happened, and in English! Reception was not very good either and I got so filled with American patriotism that I very nearly became the so-called 'ugly American.' I felt embarrassed that my island still seemed so backward, a feeling I have regretted ever since. I expressed snobbishness and did not convey the happy exultation that I had wanted to on this memorable achievement.

On another day I went to the Sliema Promenade, which remains a favorite place to enjoy the sea breeze on summer evenings. On one side of the walkway is the beautiful Mediterranean Sea and on the other side are hotels, restaurants, apartments and shops. I strolled along, searching for the baths I used to love, carved in the rocky shore with access to the sea. Each one of these baths was about 25 square feet and proportionately deeper than the next. I remember children would wade in the first one, go waist-deep in the second, swim freely in the third, be neck-deep in the fourth and jump or dive into the fifth. Sometimes a group would rent a tent-like screen for privacy. These portable partitions were large and fitted around the pool, standing about ten feet high. They had no top to them so the sun could still shine through and down on to the water.

I have very happy memories of this area where my mother would bring my siblings and me when we were young. She'd pack a delicious lunch and we would picnic and play in the water. I'd watch as the sea entered through a narrow break in the rock, swelled the pools, climbed the shallow walls, and receded out again. Sadly, now as I looked at them, they seemed to be in a neglected state. Further down the shore, I saw that many beachgoers were enjoying a new attraction with modern playground areas, snack bars, showers and other conveniences. The baths had been replaced and forgotten and only some nostalgic souls like me still eased into the enticing and refreshing waters, recalling our childhood.

Over the years I have had many occasions to return to Malta. Each time I appreciate the island's culture, food, family traditions, religious beliefs and moral values that were instilled in me while growing up. I remain very grateful to my adopted country, the good old USA, for its freedoms and great opportunities it has provided me through some hard times. Both cultures have sustained me.

Chapter Fourteen

Worsening Illness

I returned back home from my visit to Malta to a pleasant surprise. While my daughter and I had been in Malta, Tony had successfully undertaken and completed the task of building a large wooden roof over our patio as he had planned. According to our teenage son who had helped in the endeavor, many swear words were embedded with the nails! Still it was tremendously appreciated.

Every little or big thing my husband managed to do filled me not only with joy, but also with the elusive hope that he would eventually get better. Although he still had problems with his eye and numbness on the whole right side of his face, his physical strength seemed to have been regained. I tried my best to encourage him. I love to cook and made sure he ate well-balanced meals. He continued his electric stimulation exercises which gave me reason to believe that he was improving, but I neglected, or denied, or refused to see that his mental state continued to lapse into the belief that he was being constantly watched and spied on by his enemies, whomever he believed they were.

It all came to a head one early evening in late 1969 when he demanded that I accompany him to a doctor in Beverly Hills. He had been wanting me to do this for a while, trying to convince me that the medical doctors at the Orange County Medical Center were all against him and were taking orders from the F.B.I. He believed they all wanted to get rid of him because, as he put it, he knew about the toxicity of paints and he was on to something that they did not want him to find out, so he had to be stopped. He became more agitated and insisted that he must go to Los Angeles and find a doctor who agreed with him and would support him in filing the necessary forms of complaints.

That day I got the courage to stand up for myself. Maybe because I was tired, maybe because I knew what the doctor would really say or even maybe because I kept hoping that my husband would be able to finally see the futility of what he had been doing. I was the only one working and supporting the family and I could not justify paying another two to three hundred dollars to an expensive doctor, to be told, as many times before, that Tony needed psychiatric help. I decided I would not be an enabler anymore. I told him that I was not going to go with him to any more doctors and that I had no intention of missing a day's pay. He had to go by himself or accept the fact that he had a brain tumor and that it had been removed.

Yes, I agreed he still had some pain and a few disabilities, but he could continue to get better if he stopped believing that there was a conspiracy against him. I did not mean to sound cruel, but agreeing with his fantasies had not helped before and I felt we had reached the point where I needed to take a stand.

I was in the living room and he was close by, near the hallway leading to the bedrooms. Mariane, 10-years-old then, had just entered the dining/kitchen area off the living room. Obviously upset with my strong words, Tony swiftly turned and stomped down the hallway towards the master bedroom. Tears swelled in my eyes and I wondered if I was doing the right thing. How long was this chaos going to last? Every day I came home from work and listened to his tirade against doctors, against people in general, against the police and the F.B.I. He was suspicious of everyone. To be honest, all the doctors did was ply him with pills, some of which he took and some of which I saw him spit out. He refused psychological therapy so there was not much else that they could do. Dianne once told me that she preferred to be with her friend's family more than ours. I did not blame her for feeling that way, but it hurt me to hear her say it. How could I end this dilemma? He was my husband, their father, and he was a very sick man.

Our other children were working on this day, Jesse at his after-school job as a box-boy at Alpha Beta supermarket and Dianne was next door babysitting. Tony reappeared at the hallway entrance with his eyes full of rage. He crouched, commando style, knees bent and arms apart. That is when I shockingly noticed that he held a large jack-knife in his right hand. For a few seconds I became rooted to the spot frozen with fear. I felt that I was going to die. We had both reached the point of no return. He was literally striking out at me in his helplessness and frustration as I suddenly and strongly came to the realization that I could no longer support his bizarre behavior. At that instant Mariane started towards me from the kitchen and my motherly protective instinct took hold. In a most unexpected way, I did not see him as my husband, for-better-or-for-worse, but as a sick man who could kill me and maybe even our children.

I quickly became very aware that I had to do something. Our condition had deteriorated to a life-and-death situation and I had to protect my children and myself. I reached out and grabbed Mariane's hand and darted for the front door. In a chance of fate, my husband lurched up from his squatting position, turned around and with full force stabbed the hallway door three times, each time imbedding the knife to its hilt. He then collapsed in a heap on the floor, sobbing.

This time I did not go to him. I pulled Mariane with me as we ran next door where Dianne was, not noticing that Tony had followed us. I ran to the phone to call the police, but before I could dial, my husband's hand was on the receiver. He returned the phone to its cradle and firmly declared,

"I am leaving, I will pick up some clothes from the house and I will take your car, as it is more reliable."

He then took hold of Mariane, pulled her towards him and took her with him back towards our house, saying,

"I am taking Mariane with me back to the house and I do not want you to call the police. I will not be taking her with me."

He seemed unaffected and calm, very different from my panicked state. I stood there shaking not knowing what to do. I reasoned that if I upset him it would make things worse and I did not want to anger him while he held Mariane. Before he left, Tony then demanded that Dianne and I leave the neighbor's house and stay against the wall between the two houses where he could see us from the window. I was still shaking and feeling cold and Dianne offered to go into the house and get me a sweater. Tony refused, assuming that she might try to use the phone.

As the minutes went by I began to fear that he might change his mind and take Mariane with him wherever he was planning to go.

About ten minutes later we saw Tony jump into my Maverick and take off. We ran inside the house to find Mariane scared but unharmed. I searched our bedroom and found that Tony had emptied his underwear drawer, taken some pants and shirts and also the little cash we kept in a top drawer. I then called my son at work, explained what happened and urged him to come home right away. I needed his support. Dianne returned next door to the kids in her care. Thankfully, it did not take long for Jesse to quickly walk the six blocks to our house.

I had no idea where Tony was going. That night I was immensely relieved that the kids and I were safely together. I do not even remember what we did after that, as we were all too stunned. We stared at the hallway door with its three large knife gashes in it and thanked God it was not any of us. We all went to bed in a bewildered state. I had no idea what my husband planned to do and our children did not know if they would ever see their father again. It was a forerunner of more tumultuous times to come.

I woke up in the middle of the night, restless and unable to return to sleep. My mind raced, trying to cope and find a way out of our predicament. This ordeal with the knife haunted me. I feared that he might come back and hurt us. As dawn approached, I decided to call my brother Joe in Canada. He was the closest relative and, while being the younger brother, he had somehow taken it upon himself to be the head of the family in times of need. His siblings would consult with 'brother Joe' when confronting any serious decisions. In fact we jokingly referred to him as 'The Godfather.'

Canada time is three hours ahead, so when I called him early the next morning, he had just finished his breakfast and was getting ready to leave for work. I had only meant to tell him what happened and ask him for advice, but as I relived the experiences of the previous evening and voiced my fears, I crumbled. Pent-up emotions took hold of me and vented themselves in a flood of tears. My brother realized the seriousness of the situation and, unable to calm me down, promised that he would take the next flight out of Toronto and be with me in California by late afternoon.

I called in a sick day at work, excused my children from school and we all piled into our old Ford station wagon in a desperate move to avoid my husband should he decide to return home. I drove to my long-time friend's house in Mission Viejo and by the time we got there her husband Harry had already left for work. Mary welcomed us, but as I related to her what Tony had done she advised me to take my car and hide it at a church parking lot down the street. It turned out to be a very wise decision.

We were quietly sharing lunch, deep in our thoughts, when we heard a loud knocking at the front door. We looked at each other and knew who it was. Mary and Harry's house is big with lots of windows and a large sliding door leading to the back patio. As the pounding on the door continued, we locked the sliding door and we all hid, first behind the curtains and then up the stairs, afraid that Tony would come around the back of the house and peer in. I felt very bad that I had placed my dear friend in this dire situation, but in my distraught mind she had been my only refuge. Finally the banging stopped. Since he had not seen my car, he eventually must have believed that no one was home and left. We stayed hidden for a while before we felt safe enough to venture back to the kitchen. In late afternoon, I drove my children back to Anaheim and to the Disneyland Hotel parking lot to await the Airport bus that was bringing my brother.

Just seeing Joe gave me a great emotional relief even though I really did not know what he could do to ease the trauma. Hugging him in welcome and aware of his arms around me made me feel less lost, less alone. The children were glad to see him too. I can't imagine what they must have been thinking. They too must have had hopes that somehow my brother could help us in this alarming situation. On the way home we stopped for a quick dinner while I brought him up to date about our concerns, our fears and my utter despair as to how to deal with the situation.

Later at home as Joe and I were having a cup of tea and wondering where Tony could be, the opening of the front door announced his arrival. I had refrained from changing the door locks because I still feared to upset him. This was his home too and I badly needed to hang on to hope that while here lived a man who could turn violent, it was only because he suffered from an illness… and somehow we could help him.

Yes, I was still haunted by the fear of him killing me, but I kept trying to find excuses as to why I should help him and not leave him. I refused to face the fact that maybe he was beyond help. Still, I was very glad that my brother was with us when Tony came back as I am not sure how dangerous the outcome would have been had he not been there.

Tony was greatly surprised to see Joe and immediately resented his presence. He accused him of meddling in our private affairs. I explained that I had been the one who had phoned and asked for his assistance. I tried, in the best way I could, to convince Tony that my brother had come to aid him more than to help me. To my amazement, he seemed to accept that explanation and actually thanked him for coming. Joe leaped at this opportunity and told Tony that he was eager to accompany him to the Orange County Medical Center, speak with his surgeons and try to get to the bottom of what had been troubling him for so long. Tony unexpectedly and gladly agreed but for a very different reason.

My brother wanted to learn the extent of the brain surgery performed on my husband and the prognosis of his health. He also wanted to know if Tony needed psychiatric help and what could be done to protect the family. My husband had only one thing on his mind, to convince Joe that the doctors were trying to kill him and that the F.B.I. knew the real reasons and were in on the plan. Tony still believed that because he had worked with paints, at times in areas with inadequate ventilation, he had uncovered a coast-to-coast labor safety omission that the doctors wanted to cover up. At times, I too questioned whether or not working in such conditions had contributed to his tumor, but unfortunately he had resorted to such extremes that now it was his mental health that had become the main issue. Neither Joe nor Tony voiced any apprehension the next morning as they went to the car and proceeded to drive to the O.C.M.C.

When they arrived at the hospital his doctors agreed to meet them in one of the consulting rooms. They patiently explained to my brother that surgery had been required to remove an acoustic neuroma. They told him of the resulting complications and the need for a second surgery. They agreed that Tony's emotional state had not stabilized in spite of several medications, but that his physical health had been restored. They also emphasized that Tony had continued to stubbornly reject his diagnosis and refused psychiatric help.

This was explained to my brother in Tony's presence and, on hearing all this, Tony became very agitated, started pacing the room and then suddenly demanded that the doctors pay him a million dollars which he felt they owed him for ruining his life and his family's stability. The doctors again suggested that he see a psychiatrist to help him come to terms with his condition and eventually help him understand that he could resume a normal life. Tony flatly refused, screaming,

"I am not crazy and you know it!"

The doctors looked at each other and then at my brother and shook their heads in a helpless gesture. Joe related to the doctors that Tony had threatened me with a knife and, not knowing what else he could do, did his best to calm Tony down and eased him into a chair.

While standing up again and waving his arms in the air, Tony shouted,

"See how they all support each other and do not admit what they did to me!"

While the doctors watched in silence, Joe soothingly managed to guide him out of the hospital and drove him home.

Now aware of the knife episode and seeing firsthand my husband's condition, the doctors apparently had decided to notify the police. Less than half an hour after Joe and Tony returned home, a police car pulled up in front of our house. On seeing the police car, Tony made a dash for the backyard and before the police had reached the front door he had amazingly leaped like a gazelle over the eight-foot brick wall at the back of the yard and into an apartment complex behind. My brother opened the front door and as we told the officers what happened one of them asked me if my husband was armed. Suddenly concerned about his safety, I cried out,

"No, No, please don't hurt him." Then I remembered and added,

"He might be carrying his jack-knife."

One of the policemen returned to his cruiser and the other one stayed in the house with us. He unfolded some papers and informed me that I would have to sign them so that Tony could be committed for a 72-hour observation period at the mental ward of the hospital. My brother agreed that I should do so as someone might get hurt otherwise. Reluctantly and tearfully I signed the papers.

Soon I learned that my husband had been picked up in front of the apartment building behind our house and that the officers had driven him back to the hospital where he was placed in the mental ward. Feeling that now I was safe with my husband under observation and hopefully being taken care of, Joe took the next flight back to his home in Canada.

The following morning, I was allowed to visit Tony. He appeared glad to see me but soon started complaining that the staff nurses gave him plastic utensils instead of the usual stainless steel ones. I explained to him that some patients may be inclined to hurt themselves or others and that the plastic forks and knives were issued to everyone in the ward as a precautionary measure and not just to him. He was not satisfied with my explanation. He said that he was sure that the plastic knife, fork and spoon were given to him so that the hot food and scalding coffee would melt some of the plastic and add to the poisons they were already giving him through his medication. I then asked him if a doctor had seen him yet and his response was,

"Yes, I have been seen by one of my enemies."

No doctor ever talked to me to explain how they planned to treat my husband and I was too naive to ask. At that time I always trusted that the doctors knew what they were doing. I left the hospital feeling very disillusioned and wondered what would happen when the 72 hours of observation were over. I did not have to wonder long.

Chapter Fifteen

Desperation

That same day, as my children and I were finishing lunch, a police officer again came to the door. I assumed he wanted to ask me some questions, though I was worried and curious as to why a doctor had not called me rather than send the police. With pulse racing I opened the door. The officer looked at me with apparent concern,

"Mrs. Marlin," he said, "we have just learned that your husband has escaped from the mental ward and may be on his way here. For your family's protection we suggest you leave the house and take your children away, maybe to a double-feature movie. By that time we will hopefully apprehend him. Come by the police station before you return home."

I never asked or learned how he managed to escape. My main concern now was our safety. I quickly gathered my children together and we all got in the car and headed towards the theater.

I have no recollection as to what movies we saw. I do not remember seeing anything; my eyes were either shut tight in an effort to obliterate the events taking place or blurred with tears as I faced my family's disintegration.

Fears mounted at the possibility that Tony would decide to take revenge on me for signing the papers to commit him to the hospital's psychiatric ward. When I had seen him that morning his manner had not been hostile towards me, but then again neither had he given me any indication that he had been planning to escape. By the time we left the show, the sky had turned dark.

I drove to the Stanton Police Station and two officers followed me home. They entered the house ahead of me, searched each room including the closets and under the beds. They checked the garage too and when they felt that all was safe, we were then told we could go in. They had not yet been able to locate my husband, but the house was apparently secure. Since they did not find Tony there, the officers left. I had no money for us to stay at a motel, besides, how long would we have to hide? Where else could we go? I did not want to involve my friend Mary again in this unpredictable situation, so we stayed at the house.

It was the middle of the night when Tony returned. I had not been able to sleep and easily heard the doorbell. I knew it would be him because this time he had no key. I peeked through the window curtains. His hair was disheveled and he seemed out of breath. He was clutching at the doorknob. Again I felt compassion and overcame my fears. As soon as I opened the door he limped inside. He said he had walked all the way from the hospital, a distance of about ten miles. He hardly spoke another word and neither did I, though the tears running down my face must have said a lot. As he quietly changed his clothes, removed his dress shoes and replaced his socks, I could see bleeding blisters on his feet. Then I said,

"The police and the doctors are looking for you."

He said, "I know, I am not staying here."

Without another word he walked towards the front door and then turned back,

"I need the keys to the station wagon."

I gave them to him scared of what he might do if I refused.

"Where are you going?" I meekly asked.

"Away." he simply said.

I watched him get in the car and drive away. I then sat down in a stupor. Where was my husband, the father of my children, what had become of him? Who was this man that I did not know anymore and who did not seem to know us either? I wanted my life back. I could still remember the dreams I once had. This was not what I wanted, but things just happened beyond my control and I had to deal with them, even though most of the time I felt my life slipping away.

The next morning I went to work before my children awoke. They made their own breakfasts and left for school with the lunches that I had prepared the evening before. I do not believe that they had heard their father come in that night. If they did, they never mentioned it. We were all deep in our own little worlds going through the functions of everyday life, careful around each other not wanting to open any emotional door that might crumble us. Each of us was in our own little protective cell not knowing how to express our fears, building a safe wall by staying silent. As their mother, I had not been fully there for them. I was so engrossed in protecting them from physical harm and so confused in my own feelings that I neglected to consider their emotional needs. We all knew that we were going through a very sad and troublesome time, but we all kept it inside and somehow survived from one day to the next.

The phone rang two days later about six o'clock in the evening after I had retuned home from work and the children were home from school. It was Tony. He told me that he was parked at the Alpha Beta shopping center where Jesse worked. He instructed me to take him a change of underwear and the money that he knew I had hidden in the house for emergencies. He then sternly warned me not to call the police. His plan was that I go to the shopping center, locate the station wagon, put the clothes and the money on the front seat and then enter the market. He again warned me and said that he would be watching. This time I called the police.

Within a few minutes two officers arrived. I had already begun to wonder if calling them had been the right thing to do. After explaining to them what had transpired, my anxiety rose to the degree that I felt I was about to faint. I expressed my confusion and begged them not to follow me too closely so that Tony would not guess that I had called them. I hoped he'd think that the police presence was the result of a routine search for him issued by the mental facility, which incidentally I doubted or they would have found him by now. I described the vehicle, including that it was green with a cream-colored top.

My son came with me in my car. The police kept their distance for which I was grateful; in fact, they turned down a side street to delay their arrival at the market by a couple of minutes. When Jesse and I reached the market parking lot, we were shocked to find out that the station wagon had been repainted white! We only recognized it by the year model and the license plates. As directed I put the money and the clothes on the passenger-side seat that had been left unlocked. We then hurried into the market. By the time we exited from the opposite door, the car had disappeared. The police never even had a chance to make the arrest. I learned later that he had been watching us from a phone booth. When the police voiced their disappointment, I had very mixed feelings. I was glad that I had called them but also grateful that Tony had left without finding out that I had notified them.

The next five days went routinely by, but on the sixth day Joe called to let me know that Tony had showed up at his house in Oshawa, Canada, and had blamed him for his commitment to the mental ward. This proved to be terrible news to hear, not only because Tony had found a way to cross the border with no consequence, but also that my dear brother who had come to help me was now involved and his family exposed to my husband's accusations and tantrums.

While in Canada, Tony again started visiting numerous doctors in his vain attempt to find a physician who would agree with his own diagnosis of paint poisoning and a cover-up plot. My brother was a well-known feature reporter at the *Toronto Star* newspaper and, prior to that, had been a reporter with the *Oshawa Times*. My husband had told the doctors that he was Joe's brother-in-law, that he was staying with his family and that Joe would be paying for his medical bills. The doctors had no reason to suspect otherwise and by the time they all realized what had happened, Tony had left. He phoned me one time and when I asked him if he was calling from Canada he quickly hung up saying,

"The F.B.I. surely have your phone tapped and are listening to our conversation." The F.B.I. would have had a good laugh if they knew!

Tony and I still had a joint saving's account in Canada. The buyer of our house was making monthly payments into this account that had been set up for this purpose. At that time in Canada, a seller sold his house directly to a buyer and the papers were signed at a lawyer's office. No escrow or loan company got involved. We had planned to leave the money to accumulate for emergencies, educational use or for retirement needs. Now, knowing that my husband must be close to running out of the money that I had given him, I suspected that he would go to the bank and withdraw money from the account or even close it. We had about five thousand dollars, which at that time was a good amount. It was our only savings and I needed to protect it for my family.

In desperation I drove to the Crystal Cathedral in Garden Grove and asked for help from the Reverend Robert Schuller. He instructed me to go and see a lawyer friend of his in the city of Orange, about 12 miles away. Reverend Schuller must have called him, because I was expected when I arrived. This lawyer recommended that I call the bank and tell them to close the joint account and move the funds into a new account in my name only. He said I should let them know that I would be sending them a signed letter of confirmation by express mail. He then advised me to call my brother and ask him to go and explain the situation to the bank manager. This attorney could see that I was in a distraught state and though I had been more concerned about seeking help than with his fee, I was tremendously grateful that he did not charge me anything. While I wondered how Tony would survive when he ran out of money, my primary focus was on protecting the children and myself now.

About two weeks later I was talking to Dianne in the girls' bedroom about our plans for a day at the beach. She was lying on her bed and I stood facing her with my back to the bedroom door. I saw her eyes open wide as she said in a very low voice,

"Mom, Dad is behind you."

As I turned around to face him he immediately started yelling, accusing me of taking the money from our Canadian account. That is when I knew for sure that he had in fact tried to withdraw the money and apparently had not been successful. My intervention had worked. I tried to explain to him as calmly as I could that the money had not been moved from the bank and that I had only placed it in a separate account to safeguard it. I then told the kids to get ready as we were going to the beach as planned.

As we were getting our things together he followed us around the rooms saying nothing. It was like the quiet before the storm. I hurriedly piled blankets, folding chairs and the ice-chest into the car trunk. I did not know what he was thinking or planning to do, but to be safe my main concern now involved getting the children and myself out of the house and into a public place.

We got in the car and headed down Beach Boulevard towards Huntington Beach. We saw him get in the station wagon and follow us. It was almost surreal, me driving and my three children turning their heads from side to side and backwards looking out the car windows to see if he was still behind us and every few seconds whisper,

"I can still see him. He is still there."

It was my husband, their father, whom we were trying to get away from. What do I do now? How was this going to end? Will it ever end? I rode an emotional roller coaster that kept going round and round and up and down, and I did not know how to make it stop. I tried hard to concentrate on my driving, but I could not shut out my children's voices as they kept nudging each other,

"He is still behind us."

What were they thinking? Had they sensed my anxiety that I had tried so hard to hide and now were afraid of their own father? I had often emphasized that he was not a bad man but a sick man and that he too had been hurting. Yet deep inside I knew that he could hurt us; that was the reality now and somehow I had to find a way out of this situation.

We reached the beach with him right behind us. We parked, gathered our beach gear and found a nice sandy area to lay everything down. We had barely sat down when we saw him approaching. I tried to pretend that it did not matter; after all, we were in an open area with swimmers and sunbathers all around us. What could he possibly do? I coaxed my children to go for a dip in the ocean, but they did not want to leave my side. They huddled in silence. Then to my astonishment and disbelief I watched as Tony started circling our blanket like a vulture waiting for the spoils. He began by yelling a litany of accusations. Pointing a finger at me and in an audible voice to everyone around, he accused me of siding with the doctors instead of believing that he was poisoned, of turning our children against him, of stealing the money from our joint account and of being brainwashed by the American social workers. With everybody in the vicinity staring at us I became very nervous and restless. I could not ignore him anymore. He left me no choice but to again pack everything up, load the car and drive back home.

My children and I did not say one word on the way home. We were each in a little cocoon not knowing what to say or think or do.

I again tried to concentrate on driving safely home while wondering what would happen once we got there. The silence between us seemed paralyzing, none of us daring to say anything, afraid that any word could cause us to recoil in fear and we would lose our strong facade. I thought of driving to the police station, but again the horror that he might hurt us if I upset him overwhelmed me. The fact that I had three children depending on me did not allow me to risk a confrontation. We arrived home emotionally exhausted and were relieved not to see his car. We silently prayed that he would not return… but he did.

Just a few minutes after we entered the house he showed up. I do not remember what time it was, but we had not had lunch and the kids were getting hungry. I managed to make some soup and sandwiches for us all while Tony and I debated over and over about the problems we were facing. I had to watch what I said because any suggestion that he needed to see a psychiatrist would have upset him and sent him into a rage again.

Later, I turned the television on to distract the children and a spy show came on. My husband's agitation increased, as he believed that all the spy and detective stories were intentionally sending him messages through the TV. He started kicking the set and I quickly turned it off and sent the kids to their rooms. Fortunately, in their confused state they meekly obeyed and hurried off. Tony lingered and did not seem in any hurry to leave.

I had to get up at five in the morning to get ready for work, so I told Tony that I had planned to go to bed early as I felt very tired. I had hoped he would leave but instead he said that it was his intention to sleep at the house that night. I then realized how afraid of him I had become as he apparently planned to sleep in our bed. Here I was in a house with three children and a sick and possibly violent man whom I had loved but now feared. I also knew that nobody could help us because nobody knew that he was at the house. Overcome with apprehension, I slid a pair of large scissors under my pillow.

Later as I lay in bed with him beside me I hardly dared to move. I closed my eyes, but I could not and did not want to sleep. No matter how tired I became, my senses seemed to sharpen and my whole body was on alert trying to anticipate his movements. I then felt his hand slide under my pillow and find the scissors. How did he know? Had he seen me put them there or merely suspected?

"Why are you keeping a pair of scissors under your pillow?" he asked.

I said nothing and kept my eyes closed. I don't know if I wanted him to think I was asleep or I really just did not want to see what he might do. In a soft voice he asked,

"Are you afraid of me? I would not hurt you."

I recalled the day he had pulled the knife and threatened me and I remained still with my eyes closed.

For the rest of the night I lay there waiting seemingly endless hours for morning to arrive. I do not know if he slept or not. I tried to build an invisible wall between us. My thoughts and feelings were completely involved with survival. I had never felt this vulnerable before and when my alarm clock finally went off, it was as if the "National Guard" had arrived.

I got up, showered and made my breakfast while he remained in bed. I contemplated the fact that I might have to leave the house while the children were still asleep and Tony was still at home with them. I thought of waking them up and silently taking them out of the house, but to my surprise Tony suddenly entered the kitchen fully dressed and ready to go. I asked him what he planned to do and where was he going. He said,

"I am leaving with you so you can drive me to my car."

After pouring him some tea and making him a piece of toast, I got ready to leave for work. We both entered my car and to my amazement, instead of seating himself on the passenger seat, he crouched on the car floor, still afraid that the F.B.I. or the local police might be looking for him. In a way I could understand his fear as he was still on the run, but in reality nobody was actually looking for him. By that time I had become convinced that my children and I were really on our own.

He told me to drive one block to the main road and turn right on the first street, where he had left his car in the parking lot of the apartment complex. He told me when to stop and then he jumped out of my car and ran into his. As I drove away a big sigh of relief escaped my lips. As I reached the hospital I called the kids to let them know I was fine and wish them a good day at school. I thanked God that they had no idea what my night had been like.

Chapter Sixteen

Continuing Trauma

It was about two weeks later that I received a phone call from one of Tony's doctors at the Orange County Medical Center. Apparently Tony had phoned them, used some harsh words and even threatened them. They had managed to keep him on the line while the call was being traced. The police picked him up at a phone booth in Downey, near Los Angeles. The doctor had called to let me know that my husband had been admitted to the State Mental Hospital in Norwalk, about ten miles away.

My son and I visited him that evening. Jesse was 17 years old now and I found myself leaning on him for emotional support, though it upset me when friends told him that he was the man in the family now. I felt that was a heavy burden to place on a young teen.

Driving to the hospital, I had very conflicting thoughts. On one hand, I felt relieved that I knew where Tony was and clung to the hope that he would receive the help he needed. However, thinking of him locked up in a mental hospital made me shudder. The man who had brought me from a war-torn island to this land of opportunity had been reduced to being medicated and confined almost like a prisoner.

Did he have any control over this? I wondered. *Was his stubborn refusal to admit that he had surgery for a brain tumor, and had not been poisoned, merely defiance or had the brain tumor caused enough damage to distort his reasoning? Was he a victim of circumstance or was it just his obstinate behavior that was destroying any hope of a normal life? Even under either of these conditions, wouldn't one want to do all they can to get well again?* As these thoughts rambled through my mind I was shamefully oblivious to what my son must have been feeling, having to visit his father under these conditions.

As we were ushered into the men's ward, I came face to face with the reality of it all. I saw patients walking slowly while talking to themselves. Others were shuffling by, stopping at intervals then dragging further on. A few were sitting in chairs and playing cards and some just stared blankly into space. They all seemed to be medicated. I began to contemplate the utter waste of these isolated lives. Will they get better or are they destined to spend their days forever in this desolation? I did not want to believe that my husband belonged here. Surely this had to be only a temporary setback. Then we saw him...

Tony was standing, evidently alert, talking with one of the male attendants. The nurse had probably been telling him that he had visitors. As we watched, he started walking across the room at a strong and steady pace and then he saw us. His composure immediately changed and he began to stagger. He walked towards the wall and leaned against it, steadied himself and again took a couple of staggering steps. He looked like a drunken sailor. My son grabbed my arm and we both knew that this scenario was played for our benefit. As Tony reached my side he put his head to my ear and whispered,

"Get me out of here, they are killing me."

He could have won an Oscar, but this time both my son and I had seen through his act. How sad to see a beautiful mind become ravaged like that, trying to prove to us and to himself his belief that doctors were trying to poison him. Yet he was able to mentally plan this pretense of disorientation. He knew what he was doing. He very well had intended to deceive us; so when does the mind lose its control and drift into distraught behavior? I could not digest all the implications. We spent our visit mostly in silence, as we sat in chairs facing each other, fidgeting. When we left, both my son and I understood that his father's well-being was beyond our words of comfort. He needed more than we could give him.

The next day after work, I again went to visit him. This time he was more talkative and told me that when the police picked him up they had also confiscated his car. I had not even thought about the whereabouts of the car, having been so distraught with all the goings-on. He suggested I go and reclaim it as soon as I could because we were being charged storage fees. Through officers I had come to know at the Stanton Police Department, I learned that the station wagon was at a salvage yard in Downey. A friend from work drove me there the following day. I had to pay $75 in storage fees, which at that time was a lot of money for me, but I figured it was worth taking it home so that Tony will have a car to drive after his release from the hospital.

The vehicle had accumulated a lot of dust and Tony's dirty clothes were in the back seat. That weekend I decide to clean it up. It seemed as if washing it somehow erased its tainted history, but more importantly my neighbors would not wonder and question where it had been. I dreaded having to answer the anticipated inquires though my neighbors were very solid in their support.

After putting Tony's dirty clothes in the washing machine and hosing the car down, I opened the trunk. I found a small ice cooler, some rags and a few car tools that were strewn around haphazardly. Wanting to make sure I did not miss anything, I then opened the spare tire cover and there in the wheel well, were two .45 caliber guns and ammunition.

With heart pounding, I drove the car to the Stanton Police Department. Lt. Jim Brown, who had become my friend through all this confusion, took possession of the guns and ammunition and gave me a receipt. He later informed me that they had been stolen from a gun show and had been returned to their owners. The authorities never charged my husband with this theft, since he was considered psychologically disabled and in a mental hospital. Charging him would have been futile.

That same weekend, my son and I drove to a rooming house in Long Beach where Tony told us that he had been renting a room. We picked up his few belongings and amongst them we found a large book diagramming and describing the workings and use of a collection of guns. Tucked between the pages we found a handwritten list of doctors and lawyers under the heading, "My enemies."

The next two months went by uneventfully. Tony was kept on medication and compelled to attend counseling sessions. Feeling lost and exhausted, I struggled to balance my time between my nursing job, visiting him, taking care of home and children, and trying hard to sleep each night. I should have been encouraged by the way things were going, that he finally was having some counseling. But I had been conditioned by so many previous reversals and unexpected turns of events that Tony had sprung on me. Instead of expecting him to get better, I prepared myself for a call from the hospital telling me that he had escaped again or that his actions had required them to call the police or place him in isolation. I never knew exactly what to expect anymore and by now a positive outcome did not seem possible.

I did my best to continue visiting him after work as often as I could. We did not talk much on these visits. I had begun to feel pessimistic and he clammed up. If I asked him how he was doing or how things were going, he would give me a half smile, but his eyes would tell me otherwise. His smile began to look like a sneer. I could sense that he was still trying to manipulate my feelings and it was pitiful seeing him like that. It is hard to explain, but I started to see him differently. I could not escape the loneliness, sadness and loss, but by now I had also acquired the protective guard of self-preservation, being fully aware that in his mind he was capable of doing things that could hurt me. I guess in a mixed up way he too acted from behind a self-defensive need. Since he strongly believed that he never had a tumor but had been poisoned by the paints he had worked with, he was ready to strike out against anyone who disagreed with him, including me.

We now began to lock horns. He did not see me as his wife any longer but as part of the establishment that he feared. He convinced himself that the medical doctors, the psychiatrists, the police and even society in general had indoctrinated me. He saw me, if not as a direct enemy, surely as a brainwashed ally of his foes. He did not trust me.

As for me, I started to see him as he really was. I put aside my dreams, my hopes, and my prayers for a miracle and accepted the fact that he was a sick man who for some reason or another wouldn't or couldn't get better and who, in a fit of anger or desperation, might injure himself or me.

Jesse asked to join me again on the next visit to see his father. We went a little later than usual because of his after-school job. Tony had not expected us at that hour. As we entered the ward the nurse happened to be passing out routine medications. My son and I both saw him take the medicine, move to a corner of the room and spit the pills out. How long had he been doing this? I did not even feel the need to report it, as I had already resigned myself to the fact that no one was going to be able to change things. When a person does not want to be helped, he will find a way to avoid it.

I knew he was sick, but he was also dangerous since he was mentally unstable. Physically he had regained his health aside from his eye problems and he definitely had more strength than me. I always had to try to anticipate his next move. I had to work on a way to survive for the children's benefit and myself. It was a battle of wits now.

A few weeks later I received a phone call from the hospital informing me that the doctors had decided that Tony had improved enough to be released. When I arrived at the hospital I was ushered into an office and met by a social worker and a nurse. The social worker explained that Tony had been doing much better. That he seemed to be willing to accept his responsibilities and that he had also voiced regret for past behavior… and they believed him. They felt that they could now release him home on medication. They must have summoned him soon after I arrived because Tony came into the office dressed and ready to leave. He appeared reserved, but I could not help wondering what storm simmered beneath his calm appearance.

The nurse handed me a bag that contained three medicine bottles and in front of Tony she said to me,

"Make sure he takes his medications on schedule and if he gives you any trouble call us and we will come and pick him up."

I could hardly believe that she actually said this in front of him. Maybe it was their way of warning him or something to do with patients' rights. I saw Tony stiffen, then nervously shuffle in his seat. This responsibility scared me, but I did not want to voice my fears in front of him. I felt that putting me in this position of enforcing his medication actually endangered me, as it would fuel Tony's perception of me being in alliance with his enemies.

So this was to be my next challenge. I prayed that I would be able to handle it even though I had begun to feel that God did not hear me. I had bought a statue of St. Jude and placed it in my garden. St. Jude is proclaimed to be the "Saint of Impossible Cases." I had prayed to both St. Jude and the Virgin Mother to intercede for me, but my prayers seemed to no avail and this burden was never going to end. I even began to doubt if there really was a God.

On the way home from the hospital Tony sat very quietly, sunk back in his seat, then he suddenly straightened himself up and said,

"So you are my keeper now, eh?"

With this statement I felt a chill surge through me.

"Tony," I calmly replied, "they want you to get better; they just need to make sure that you take your medicine so that you will continue to improve."

As if not hearing me he added in a gruff voice,

"Make sure you call them if I do not obey."

I could see right away that his coming home was not going to work. He had already started testing me and I felt too tired and too defeated to argue. Knowing that he had spit out his pills while in hospital I knew that I could not possibly force him to take them.

I still had to go to work every day, so I stocked up on groceries for him and the children to prepare their own breakfast and lunch. I did my best to make dinner a pleasant family time, but he did not want to talk about anything other than how everyone was against him. He also distrusted me even more.

One day after I placed his dinner on the table, he picked up his plate of food, went in the backyard and placed it on the patio table. He sat there watching his plate until flies came to taste his food. Since the flies did not drop dead, he became satisfied that the food had not been poisoned. This brought back a memory of when he first had his surgery. A neighbor had kindly brought us a prepared meal and after I gratefully thanked her, he took the dish from my hand and threw it all away, stating,

"It could be poisoned."

Now this was my own food he was testing. His demonstrated mistrust increased my fear of him. If he perceived me as someone who might want to kill him I was possibly in more danger than I thought. Dinners became tension-filled events. The children and I sometimes exchanged desperate and hopeless glances, but none of us dared say a word.

With me at work and the kids in school, Tony remained alone during most of the day. He spent his time reading medical books, still trying to find something that would support his beliefs. While I again wondered at times if the tumor was the result of working with the toxic paints, I still could not make myself believe that anyone was out to kill him as he wanted so much to convince us all. In the evenings he insisted on sitting by the window so he could see if the police drove by, and if they happened to do so on their routine business, he would jump up and start swearing and kicking the TV set. Then something happened that changed everything.

Chapter Seventeen

An Unexpected Decision

As days and weeks went by, Tony became more uneasy and seemed constantly on edge. He behaved like a trapped animal afraid of everyone and everything. Anything he read in the newspaper or heard on the radio or watched on TV, he twisted and personalized. If the police were looking for a fugitive then surely it must be him. If the F.B.I. were closing in on a wanted man, then they must be close by. He became progressively harder to live with.

One day in a sudden declaration, he announced that he could not live here any longer and that he had started making plans to return to Malta! This was a statement I had never expected him to make and I did not know whether to disbelieve him or to rejoice. Because of his surgeries and state of mind, Tony had not applied for his American citizenship like I had done, but as a holder of a British Passport (both Malta and Canada had been part of the British Empire) he had no problem applying for a new passport and re-entry to the island.

When first I heard of his intention, I felt dazed and then it dawned on me that this would mean the end of our marriage and the children would be losing their father.

Did he plan to ever come back? Could he?

I found it revealing that neither the children nor I attempted to convince him to change his mind and stay.

This change of events proved to be something none of us had ever thought of, although not hard to understand, since every day he had been more desperate and more scared as his emotional health continued to deteriorate. This seemed to be his drastic attempt at some relief, a final escape from those he perceived to be his persecutors. His mother, brother and sister still lived on the island and would surely welcome him back.

As I tried to absorb all this, other feelings surfaced. I would no longer be responsible for him, nor would I go to sleep every night in fear of what he might do. I would be spared his daily litany of complaints. I was losing my husband, but the torment might also finally end. His leaving was easier than we anticipated. It was also possible for him to receive his Social Security Disability Insurance Benefits in Malta. In September of 1970, my husband took a one-way flight out of Los Angeles via London, to Malta.

I felt a great emptiness as I watched the plane depart but also a sense of peaceful comfort. I don't know which feeling was the strongest. His leaving made me a single mother. Actually I had been the sole family support for over five years, but when he left his departure made it permanent. Neither of us had talked about our separation. A new feeling of relief that suddenly arose within me was something I had never thought I would feel again. We did not discuss our future apart. He just wanted to get away from the pain and his fears and I needed some peace of mind. The dark clouds were disappearing and my children and I now looked forward to some form of normalcy. Maybe finally the agony had passed, not the way we wanted it to end, but at least we could again be our old selves and try to adjust to the mixed emotions of emptiness and new beginnings. That's what we really believed.

After he left, my children and I tried to come to terms with our new situation. Our days were filled with the usual responsibilities; I went to work and they attended their respective schools. I would prepare an early dinner each day so that Jesse and Dianne could eat before they went to their part-time jobs. They loved my meals and it was a relief that I could now concentrate on the cooking without distractions. Jesse had graduated from Servite high school and was now attending classes at California State University in Fullerton. He still worked at Alpha Beta supermarket and they were very good at scheduling him around his classes. Dianne, a junior at Rosary, now also worked part-time at Norik's fast food restaurant around the corner from our house, and Mariane was twelve. Our routines did not change, but although we now had peaceful dinners and quiet late evenings, we were all coping with the void and our unspoken feelings and frustrations at the way fate had evolved. We all still had kept hoping, deep inside, that Tony would get better and our family would one day be whole again.

A day after Tony left, we received his cable that all went well and he had been reunited with his family. It was about two weeks later that we got his first letter in which he wrote about his uneventful, yet pleasant flight. In the letter he mentioned that he had been permitted to view the cockpit, something that was allowed then. There had been no fear of terrorists, nor bolted door with impenetrable steel, as we have now. Of course neither did they know that he had been a mental patient!

He told us how happy the family had been to see him and have him live with them again. We were relieved and hoped that this will work wonders for him and that maybe his new secure surroundings would aid his recovery.

The letters kept coming, one every ten days, and a new pattern began to emerge. He started insisting that I should sell our house and with the children, join him in Malta. This was another turn of events that we had not anticipated. I asked him what his plans were for our support, home and work possibilities, in an effort to see if he had any definite arrangements that we might all agree on.

The children were doing well at school and I had a steady and self-fulfilling profession. Should I have to uproot us all? I began to feel very guilty at my rejection of this prospect. We were still husband and wife and he was the father of my children. This conflict began to wear me down and I felt as if I was on a constant slow burner, not knowing when the flames would become too hot to bear. I started having panic attacks, with racing heart and dizzy spells. I began to fear that I might pass out at unexpected moments. Although I had stopped crying, I still had a hard time falling asleep at night. The responsibilities again became greater than I thought I could handle. Any decision I made affected the whole family. I really did not want to go back to Malta, but my marriage vows were choking me. I finally came to the conclusion that I could no longer do this on my own and went to see a family counselor.

My counselor advised me to salvage what I had left. He likened my concerns to a sinking ship and said that I now had to swim to shore or go down with it. He pointed out that I had been my husband's wife, nurse, support and even his advocate, but now I had to let go and save the children and myself from any more disruption and destruction of our emotional state. I knew his advice was right, but my decisions and hesitations were related to my conscience that continued to stab me. I had changed my mind so many times, torn between obligation, guilt, and doing what had to be done, but as Cervantes once said, "By the streets of 'By and By' one arrives at the house of 'Never.' "

Tony's letters continued coming on a regular basis and with each correspondence his demands and accusations increased. He started telling me that I had been influencing our children wrongly, that America did not qualify as a good place to raise them. He added that in Malta, they eventually would meet and marry young people of their own culture. What was he trying to say? That our children would not find a decent man or woman to marry here in America? I found that to be almost laughable. I kept answering his letters trying to explain that I did not feel ready to quit my job, sell the house and get the children out of school. He wrote back and told me that I could easily work as a nurse at a hospital there, also stating that the children could attend classes at the University on the island. He was receiving his Social Security Disability Insurance Benefits, which he said would be of help until I started working and our finances improved. This made me feel even guiltier than before as I had to admit to myself that, even if he was right, I really did not want to leave California and the United States.

One of Tony's letters finally sealed our fate. I thought that he would write to tell me that he had been looking for a small house or offer some other assurance that things were going to be fine. Instead, he repeated his accusations that the American doctors had duped me. He added that I was not fulfilling my wifely duties, and that if I did not join him I would even be going against my religion. I quickly realized the dangerous snake pit I had almost fallen into. As the counselor had said, I had to save what was left of my family or I too faced the danger of becoming incapacitated.

Soon after, Tony started picketing the American Embassy in Malta. On handmade posters, in huge red letters, he claimed that American doctors had ruined his life and destroyed his marriage. In one of the

signs he even referred to the doctors in California as "MURDERERS."
His photo, holding one of the signs, was plastered on the front page
of the local newspapers including the Maltese language papers *Il Hajja*
and *L-orizzont* and the English-language paper *Malta News.* My family
in Malta was well known in town and this episode added immensely to
their embarrassment.

Chapter Eighteen

Trying to End the Madness

In June of 1971, I discovered that my indoor washing machine had been leaking water and the wooden floor beneath the vinyl tiles had begun to rot. An inspection showed that besides rot and fungus the floor also had termites. This added house responsibility was so new to me at the time, and my finances so limited, that when the termite inspector explained to me what needed to be done, I burst into tears. Needless to say my reaction shocked him. Then I felt so embarrassed that I had to let him know that I was edgy because my personal life was in shambles and any little thing seemed to upset me more than it should. It turned out that he was a good family man and calmly assured me that he will take care of everything at a reasonable price and I could pay him in small monthly installments.

The extensive repair work included removing the toilet and sink of the adjacent bathroom and replacing all the wood flooring and vinyl tiles. That evening, in a fit of anger and frustration, I wrote my first irate letter to Tony.

I angrily told him that while he enjoyed swimming on the island and accused me of being disloyal to my marriage vows, he had been the one to abandon the family. He had left me with all the responsibility of raising our three children by myself, providing for their financial and emotional welfare, and now I had the extra worry regarding the upkeep of the house. I then went on to relate the problem with the rotting floor and the termites and explained how the termite inspector would be removing the bathroom flooring and how hard it was going to be to pay for it all. By the time I finished the letter my head was pounding so hard that I began to feel nauseated. I reached for my tranquilizers and my prayer book.

Removing and replacing the bathroom floors and getting rid of the termites and the fungus were ordinary home maintenance requirements and not a major disaster, but to me at that time it again seemed like my whole world kept falling apart. Things appeared to be getting out of hand. To top it all, I realized that I was overreacting and maybe losing my grip on the situation. That night I again cried myself to sleep as I had done on many nights before. I mailed the letter on my way to work the following morning. The termite man needed a week before he could begin the work, so my leaky washing machine was disconnected and I bought a secondhand one from a neighbor who was replacing hers with a new one.

A week later I received a letter from Tony by Special Delivery. He wrote that he had answered my letter as fast as he could because it was urgent for me to know that underneath the bathroom floor was a .44 Magnum handgun. He wrote that he had placed it there in case he ever returned! The termite man's delay had proved to be a blessing!

In the letter he drew a diagram showing how I could reach the gun from the outside wall if I opened the bathroom trapdoor, which led beneath the tub. Most houses have such access openings in case a plumber needs to reach below the tub for service. He guided me as to how to get a wire clothes hanger, straighten it out, bend the end into a half circle and then reach and pull the gun out that was resting between the 2x4's against the inside wall. I sat down on the kitchen chair with the letter in my hand and I could not stop shaking. Another gun where I least expected it!

What did he mean when he said he had put it there in case he returned? What was he planning to do with it? Was he planning to kill us? I wondered if these sudden and unexpected horrible surprises would *ever* come to an end.

After I calmed down, I went into my backyard and located the wall that backed up against the bathroom. There were plants in front and along the length of the wall. There behind the leaves, about a foot off the ground, was a wooden door about the size of a small manhole that the foliage had obstructed from view. It had a small latch and was easy to open. I tried to peek inside but could not get my head in far enough.

The tub and its plumbing were right in front of me and there was no space to put my whole head inside. I decided to wait until my son came home so he could help me. While waiting, I straightened out a wire hanger and looped the end into a semicircle as Tony had instructed.

When Jesse arrived home I gave him the letter to read and he became as upset, alarmed and angry as I was. After studying the situation we came up with the idea of using a mirror and trying to see if we could find the gun that way.

Kneeling on the left side on the door, I held a small compact mirror in my left hand and angled it towards the inside wall on the right. There, resting up against the wall, I could see the gun with its handle towards me. Still holding the mirror, I eased the wire in my right hand, against the wall until the rounded end reached the gun. My son was kneeling on the ground in front of me to the right of the door and could not see much, but his calm encouragement helped me to go very slow so I would not drop it.

It took about three tries before I managed to hook the wire to the handle of the gun and cautiously began to pull it towards me. Unfortunately I could not pull it beyond the 2x4 stud. It was a tight squeeze and no matter how much I tried, I could not put my head far in enough to see, so dispensing with the mirror I had to blindly reach with my left hand, feel around and pick it up. As I moved my hand it brushed against a small cardboard carton. I succeeded in getting the gun out and then retrieved the box. When I opened it, I found that it held 30 bullets; six bullets were missing.

I started to tremble and had to hold on to my son to keep myself from falling, as it dawned on me that the six missing bullets must be in the gun. I then became incredibly angry with my husband for not warning me that the gun had been loaded. The way the gun had been pointed, had I mistakenly hooked the wire to the trigger instead of the handle, I could have killed my son!

The thought of that horrible possibility gave me the strength to decide that I can't let this go on. I had to put an end to this madness. I turned the gun and the bullets over to the Stanton police, even though to be honest, I was tempted to keep it for self-defense. The following week I filed for divorce.

The actual filing process turned out to be very easy. I went to an attorney, discussed with him my situation, signed the necessary papers and started the proceedings. However, again my conscious would not let me be. Divorce is not allowed in my Catholic faith and nobody in my family had ever gotten divorced. Besides the obligations of my religious beliefs, I also wondered if my family would blame me and maybe even disown me. Thoughts also entered my mind that if I proceeded with a legal divorce, I might have to sell our house.

Then where would my kids and I go?

More than that, however, was my steadfast refusal to give in and surrender my belief that our marriage could be salvaged. I just did not want to give up. Against all odds I was reluctant to admit that my dream of a life-long union had gone astray. Facing the truth had become too painful. By the end of the following week, guilt overcame me and I went back to my attorney and cancelled the filing.

My son, seeing my conflicting dilemmas and how stressed I had become, wrote to his father and told him that the way things were at the moment he agreed with me in my decision to not make such a drastic move back to Malta at that time. Tony became very angry and wrote back an insulting letter to our son. He accused him of being a "Mama's boy" and even threatened that, had he still been in Malta where he could reach him, he would have slapped him hard.

This upset us all. I regretted that my son had to receive such degrading remarks from his own father and it hurt me to realize that, because of an illness, our children had to be subjected to these consequences. Even so, I continued to remind them that their father acted this way because he was sick and not because he did not love them. I tried hard to save them from becoming emotionally scarred.

Another week went by and both my mother and brother in Malta each sent me a letter stating that Tony had been voicing some insulting remarks at them and had even been making threatening gestures by running his hand across his throat and pointing at them. My mother had become very scared and did not want to even leave the house. My brother Ronnie had reported these episodes to the local police, but nothing much more could be done about it. With another acknowledgement of the danger he posed, I now became fearful for my family in Malta. I made another appointment with my attorney and re-filed for the divorce. This time I promised myself to see it through. Of course my husband had to be informed and to my consternation, another local attorney notified me that he was representing Tony's contesting of the proceedings.

I went to see him and found out that my husband had not told him anything about his medical or mental conditions or the reason I had filed for divorce. After he listened to what I had to say and also consulted with my own attorney, he decided that he would not take my husband's case. This infuriated Tony and in a few days I received a letter telling me that he did not care about me, did not care about our children and that we can all go to hell! My attorney apprised my husband of the pending court date and also published a notice in the Malta local paper as required by law.

When my divorce case came up in court, my lawyer used Tony's letter in my defense; my husband was not there to state his case or to introduce any arguments. Jesse and Dianne acknowledged to the judge that they wanted to remain with me and Mariane was still a minor. I cannot imagine what was going through their minds. They did not express any emotion openly. This had been going on for years and, like me, they must have felt extremely sorrowful yet relieved that this might hopefully put an end to our emotional upheaval.

The judge wanted to study the information further rather than issue an immediate decision. I had been supporting the family and making all the payments on the house. I asked for no alimony or child support, because I knew that payment would be hopeless. Following my lawyer's advise, I did request a restraining order.

Two weeks later my attorney called me with the good news that all had been approved and the judge had awarded me the house. The divorce would be final in six months and our meager savings from the house we had sold in Canada was to be divided equally between my husband and me. However, there was also a stipulation that Tony's share would be placed in a separate bank account for child support and I could withdraw from it sixty dollars a month for each child until it was exhausted. This amount only consisted of three thousand dollars so it did not last very long, though it helped.

So now I owned the house and the fear of losing it was over. Did I celebrate? Did I feel good? No! On the contrary, I was deeply heartsick that my marriage had to end this way. In reality my marriage had ended years before, but this made it legal. At least now he could no longer insist that I sell the house or that I and the kids should move back to Malta. The children and I still had a roof over our heads and I had the legal papers to support it. This was a consolation, but the fallout from the divorce had yet to be confronted.

My first return to Malta in 1969. Mariane is pictured in front of the house where I was born–the street is decorated for the upcoming religious festa.

Mariane is standing on the spiral staircase of my childhood home.

Our station wagon that Tony later disguised when he was on the lam.

Bathroom trapdoor that was hiding something sinister.

Tony, depressed and frustrated, picketing the American Embassy in Malta in Dec. 1970.

July 4 1971.

This is in answer to your last letters of the three of you, because it's not worth spending the 10d in postage stamp to each of you.

As we could'nt get the Americans to hurry with the Compensation, and we know exactly what they have been trying to do, and we can not take the American Embassy to Court because they have immunity, the lawyer has advised me to resume my picketing, or he said to me laughingly, quote. "You can always take Court Action if you go back to California, and also settle things with your wife at the same time, because we don't have divorce law here in Malta." I replied and "Who wants to go back to "HELL" for anything in the world.

Anyway the lawyer has written the Legal Aid Society in California and asked for someone to represent me from there and then we can proceed with the divorce, as soon as an attorney is appointed from there.

My "Protest" picketing at the American Embassy has re-started three days ago and my Posters so far have read.

My 1st day Poster.   My 2nd day Poster.

My 3rd day Poster.
as a reminder.

I could see that people are interested to read my posters, because I could see their lips moving and expressions on their faces. My 1st and 2nd Posters had humour in them and the people sort of smiled. But with the r 3rd day Poster, I got a frightful look on their faces. The rest of my Posters:- That is how they're going to be.

Yea you guessed right, your name is coming up soon.

TONY.

One of Tony's threatening letters.

STATE OF CALIFORNIA

DEPARTMENT OF EMPLOYMENT
MANPOWER DEVELOPMENT AND TRAINING ACT
NOTICE OF CHANGE IN ALLOWANCES PAYABLE

Name ALICE J MARLIN

STANTON, Calif 90680   Project No. R 6075

Date 2-16-6

Beginning with the week ending 1-20-67 your allowances will be adjusted as indicated below:

Training Allowance   from $ 63   to $ 68

Subsistence Allowance   from $ to $

Transportation Allowance   from $ to $

☑ Transportation allowances are subject to exclusion of first $0.50 per round trip.

Your allowances are changed for the following reason: You became Head of House hold for MDTA Purposes

If you have any questions about your training allowances, please contact the Manpower Training Specialist in the local Employment Service Office which referred you to training.
ES 950E REV. 2 (1-67)

My qualification form to enter the nursing program.

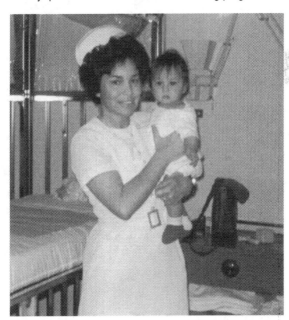

Nursing at Children's Hospital of Orange County in California 1973.

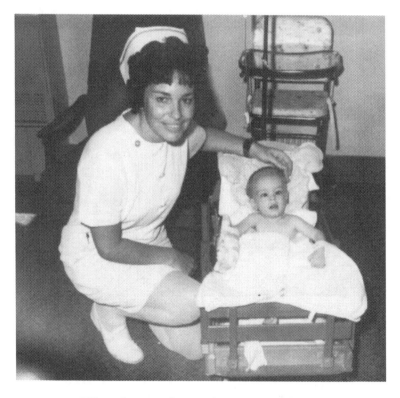

With another one of my precious patients at CHOC.

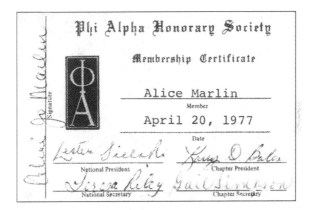

My Honorary Society card.

Dean's Honor List

The School Dean and Faculty of
California State University, Long Beach
extend Honor and Congratulations
for outstanding scholastic achievement
during the academic year to

ALICE J. MARLIN

Dean, School of Letters and Science

1974–75

Dean's Honor List recognition.

Graduation day from CSULB, on May 31st 1977.

My BA Degree—my education gave me so much more than this paper.

Me and my mother in 1972 at Huntington Beach, California.

My mom with her grandchildren, Dianne, Mariane and Jesse.

Visiting Disneyland with mom—we did our best to try to forget our sad circumstances and make her visit enjoyable.

Dianne, Mariane and Jesse in our backyard, 1966.

This picture pose became somewhat of a ritual;
here are my 3 kids again in Nov. 1970.

All grown up and striking same pose in March 2001.

My children visiting and having fun posing again in Feb. 2009.

Jesse and Ginger were married in a lovely garden ceremony at their home in 1986.

Mariane and Jim's wedding in 1989 was catered at a country club and included a live band

In 1998 Dianne and Danny were married in Malta at the same church that Tony and I were married in.

Tony's funeral in 1989. His nephew sent us photos.

Tony's grave in the Santa Maria Addolorata Cemetery, which is the main Roman Catholic cemetery on the island. My parents are also buried there.

Family gathering for my 70th birthday celebration.

Chapter Nineteen

Tony Takes Drastic Measures

When my husband learned about the outcome of our divorce and the settlement, he became enraged. In his sick paranoid condition, he again picketed the American Embassy and now warned me that *my* name would appear on his next signs. Apparently I was to be named as an ally to his doctors, brainwashed and unfaithful to him.

In my distress and in an effort to help my family, I considered going back to the island in an attempt to try and see if I could pacify Tony, reason with him and maybe bring this tumultuous period to a peaceful end. I don't know why I thought I could do this or why I would even think of putting myself in such a dangerous situation, but at that time I did not know anymore what was right or wrong... or maybe I too was losing my mind. To my credit, I decided to write to the Immigration Department in Washington D.C. and ask for advice.

They wrote back and warned me that although I had obtained an American divorce, on the Catholic island my divorce was null and void, and I would still be considered Tony's wife. They further advised me that if any demands or force was pressed upon me while in Malta, my only recourse as an American citizen was to go to the American Embassy. I will be forever grateful for their advice as their warning reinstated my sanity and I changed my mind about going.

Summer of 1971 was approaching and Jesse suggested that he would take a vacation and go on his very first visit to Malta. He looked forward to meeting his grandmothers, his uncles, aunts and cousins. He also wanted to be able to take a look at his father's condition while he was there. My heart filled with joy, as this would be a close-up look at reality.

My son showed a lot of excitement at getting in touch with his roots and seeing the island that I had told him so much about. He met the family and they made him feel very welcome. He loved the island, enjoyed the beautiful Mediterranean Sea, but came back with the somber statement that I have to forget about returning there because his father was still the same embittered, scared and very sick man.

Soon after, Tony wrote to inform me that he was planning to return to the United States! He did not offer any explanation. I was petrified. I felt my life was now at stake and in self-defense I again put pen to paper. This time I wrote to the American Embassy in Malta and to the Malta Passport Office. Besides a brief outline of the overall situation and a mention that I had obtained a restraining order against him, I emphasized that Tony could be very cunning and may use either his British or Maltese Passport. Also, since we had changed our name legally here in California, he might apply for a visa under his birth name that was still registered in his baptismal records.

The American Embassy in Malta replied and eased my fears by stating that they were very much aware who my husband was since his picketing of the Embassy and that his obtaining a visa to the United States was out of the question. I experienced relief for a few moments until I recalled how easy it had been for him to enter Canada when he had traveled there while the police were still searching for him. Surely, he could use his British passport to visit Canada again and then cross the border to the United States. With his British passport he would not need a visa to enter the U.S.A. as a tourist.

While all this was going through my mind and panic dictated my every move, my family in Malta wrote to tell me that Tony had entered the local church during Mass and had marched up and down the center aisle proclaiming he was Jesus. He had then been transported to the island's mental hospital, placed under sedation and admitted as a patient. So for a while, I was again able to maintain a fragile form of normalcy.

While Tony remained hospitalized for about three months, we did not hear from him. Then I received news from my brother and mother that he had been released from the hospital and had gone to live with his newly wed nephew John. He had been saving some money from his disability checks and managed to put a down payment on a small house. The American dollar brought a good money exchange value. Also, apparently a new medication was working in keeping him calmer.

The newlyweds, John and Teresa, would live in the house and in return take care of his household needs. Teresa kept his room clean, washed his clothes and included him at dinner. His time was his own and he spent hours walking or swimming. John and Teresa owned part of a family hobby shop and John also worked as a handyman. He was very good at carpentry, plumbing and also electrical troubleshooting. He worked at these jobs while Teresa tended the shop. This arrangement was beneficial to all of them, as John and Teresa needed new housing and Tony enjoyed having someone, especially a relative, to look after him.

He broke off all correspondence with us, which I did not mind since the previous letters had always been threatening. I regretted, however, that he never wrote to any of the children, not even on their birthdays. At Christmas, I usually received a card wishing the kids and me a happy holiday. He always signed it "your loving husband." I felt that he intentionally did this to remind me that as a Catholic, I remained his wife.

It was about this time that my mother decided to come for a visit; it would be her first time to the United States. Not only was she concerned about me, but she had never met Dianne and had only seen Jesse and Mariane briefly during their visits to Malta. She had been living alone since all her children had moved abroad to North America and my father had passed away about two years earlier.

She first visited my brother and his family in Canada and then came to spend ten days with us. I was so happy to see her and have Dianne meet her Grandmother. I took some days off from work and we spent as much time together as we could. We managed to take her to Disneyland, Knott's Berry Farm, the Deer Park, and the beach. Mother was impressed with our sandy beaches and the fact that they stretched as far as the eye can see. Although Malta is surrounded by the Mediterranean Sea, its beaches are mostly rocky and the few sandy shores are quite small.

We did our best to make her visit a memorable one while trying to forget the sad circumstances we were going through. This had been a big step for my mother, as she had never traveled alone this far before. We hoped that she returned home in the knowledge that we were holding up well and adjusting to our situation.

The months turned into a year and although our life had finally begun to proceed at a normal pace, I started to suffer from migraine headaches and sleepless nights again. After years of constant fears and unresolved emotions, I now had time to look back on past events and indulge in feeling sorry for myself.

My 40th birthday had just passed and I felt so alone, raising three kids, still in school. Money was still tight and my heart ached to see the oldest two children come from school and then go straight to their part-time jobs with no time for fun or after-school activities. They did not complain, but I knew that they were missing out on many pleasurable pastimes with their friends. I continued to seek help through counseling and, for the next eight months, I tried to learn to cope.

I loved my children dearly, but sometimes I expected too much from them and because I was so depressed myself, I did not take their feelings into consideration. When I came home from work, if I found a bed unmade or dishes left on the kitchen table, I would have a fit. I yelled at them and often scolded them. On occasion I withdrew to my bedroom in utter despair. In the isolation of the room, I tried hard to contemplate what was happening to me and why every little thing appeared like a huge obstacle to be overcome. It seemed that if anything was out of place, it triggered a flood of negative emotions in me suggesting that my life was still unraveling. If they asked me later why I had been so upset, I would again scream "Just because!" which upset them even more. I never discussed with them how I really felt or voiced my fears. In my endeavor to protect them, I was pushing them away from me again. I remembered a letter that I had found years ago on my bedside table that addressed my behavior. It was also from Dianne and here are her own words:

Dear Mom,

I have been thinking for a long time and I have decided to write you this note. The thing I would like to have most in the world is a family, but I doubt whether I will ever have dad back or not, so I have turned all my needs to you. Mom, you are all I have and I want so much for you to love me. Every time we have an argument it kills me. Believe me I always end up in my room crying and I have made a point to look for your reasons. I search and search for your point of view and sometimes I find it. I know it must bother you to come from work and find me watching TV, with ironing piled up and my bed unmade, and I am sorry.

I could have and should have done this work. Even putting aside what Mariane does, I think what I worry about most, is whether or not it's worth it. I want you to appreciate me. I won't deny that I accept an allowance for my chores, but what makes me happiest is when you appreciate my work. Haven't you noticed that it hurts me when I am doing something and instead you look at what I didn't do? It's as though I crave praise from you yet when I do something for you I am never satisfied with your praise. Maybe the only way I can get it is by you comparing me to others.

Mom, I'm a person, and as I write this I hope and pray that you do not get the wrong impressions. I DO consider myself special. I am me, and no one else can claim this. You and Dad made me what I am. You know that I am better than average. I have high goals about what I want to do with my life.

I come home and talk until doomsday, wanting to share my experiences with you. When I hear a joke I try and remember it for you. I can't be satisfied keeping everything inside myself. I know I am stubborn, but I guess once you get that way you can't change. Don't think I didn't notice that you did not yell at me last night. I respected you more because it wouldn't have done any good anyway.

I guess you were tired last night. It seems silly that a little chore should cause so much damage. I tried to talk to you. I DESPISE the answer "because." That is an answer you give to a child.

Mom, I don't want this family to go down the drain. I DO NOT want to leave when I am eighteen. Leave to what?

I am going to try and straighten up. Maybe if I do my work in a more pleasant tone, things will improve. We all have to pitch in.

Bye,

I love you,
Dianne

She was about 15 when she had written this. Yes, she was special. All of my children were special. I love them so much.

What was I doing? I knew that I said the wrong things sometimes because I felt so alone and the responsibilities were so great, but I shouldn't have taken my frustrations out on them. They had lost their father. Surely that had cost them a lot of grief, must I add to it all now by being so critical? If Dianne had told me all this vocally, I don't know if I would have heard her, but her letter, read in the stillness of my room, reached the core of my heart. "Please God," I prayed, "Help me." For the next half hour, I just sat on my bed in deep thought, clutching her letter to my heart. I had to make myself understand that the children were hurting also.

There must have been other evidence of the children's anguish that I had missed. When Mariane was only six years old, she drew a picture of a long car with all the windows darkly painted. Underneath she wrote, "This is a Hearse." Why would such a young girl in first grade draw such a morbid thing like that? It was 1965, the year her father was diagnosed with a brain tumor. Had she already feared that he might die? It is only now, as I write these memoirs, that I can stop, think and realize that I had not been the only one in pain. I had tried to shield my children, but their young, innocent eyes did not keep them from understanding or becoming aware of the truth.

In November of 1970, two months after Tony had returned to Malta, one of Mariane's pets, a black cat to which she had given the longest name ever, disappeared. We searched for him everywhere we could think of, to no avail. It was about a month later that I came across this note that she had written.

Good Morning God,

Hi! How is everything up there? Can you tell me if Dad is going to be all right? Is my cat Sumitomo Sukiaki Fujiyama I in heaven?

> *Oh I hope he is having fun. Thank you for getting rid of Mitten's infection. (our other cat) I am sure she is thankful too. I like our new neighbors, except I do not like it when their little girl Marcy wanders into our back yard.*

Mariane Marlin
St. Polycarp School
November 25, 1970

Mariane had just turned eleven when she wrote this.

I began to realize that we were having a hard time expressing our grief verbally to each other. We remained impenetrable, enclosed in our shells, keeping our sorrows private. I know that I thought that if they did not see me cry, their hurt would somehow be lessened, but the kids too must have felt personal pain. They followed my lead. The girls' expressions emerged in pictures and in letters while I cried in my writings where I poured out my feelings and explored possible solutions on most any piece of paper that I had—my school notebooks, letters, newspaper margins, etc. My son, on the other hand showed no expressed emotion. However, he had always been there for me, accepting the brunt of all my anger and fears and tried to keep the peace between his sisters when they disagreed. How I treasured all their support.

Chapter Twenty

Family Support

During one of my counseling sessions the therapist asked me to vocalize what I wanted most to do with my life. I laughed aloud.

What I wanted to do? That question had never crossed my mind. It had always been, *What would my husband do next?* or, *How am I going to pay my bill?* And now, *What will happen to my family if I get sick?* What I wanted to do had never ever been considered.

The counselor insisted and repeated the question. Feeling uneasy and nervously rubbing at my eyes, I blurted out,

"I would like to be able to work less hours so that I have more time to care for my family and maybe even return to college for one or two classes a week."

My workload at the hospital required that I give up many weekends, leaving the kids on their own. I was glad that I had the day shift, but like police officers and firemen, nurses have to be available for work 24 hours a day, seven days a week. Although I enjoyed my profession, I had begun to feel close to burnout. The responsibilities of caring for very sick children—some just out of surgery on ventilators, or even in iron lungs, others suffering from burns or injuries, and dear others fading away with leukemia—were a constant tug on my fragile emotions. Additionally, the agony of sometimes losing a child to their illness could be unbearable. Nevertheless, I loved being able to rejoice when we were able to send the little ones home fully recovered. Of course assisting in their recovery and sending them home was always our primary focus and goal. Happily, we were able to do that most of the time.

I found my job to be very fulfilling, giving support and encouragement to other mothers and receiving hugs while tending to the children's needs. My emotional turmoil would surface when I returned home each day to face my own disillusionment and emptiness. I suspect I was experiencing a post-traumatic reaction. Now that my husband was thousands of miles away, I was trying to absorb the reality of being a single mother and feared the consequences to my children's life. The counselor then asked,

"Have you discussed your concerns with your children?"

"No, of course not," I replied. "In my culture, one does not expose children to family problems if it can be helped. I do not want to burden them with my troubles. I try to protect them by crying only when they are at school or at night in the privacy of my bedroom where they cannot see me." The counselor smiled,

"Your children are now in their teens, in fact the eldest is close to twenty, and you do not think they know all that has been going on?"

"To some extent they do." I agreed, "They understand that their father is a sick man. They know that he left us and that I had to file for divorce to safeguard our home. They are aware of my day-to-day concerns, but I do not want them to know how desperate I feel or how lonely I am, or how I still sometimes cry throughout the night unable to sleep." I buried my face in my hands as I struggled with the thoughts that my fears were beginning to overwhelm me and I was losing control. He handed me a tissue and pressed me more,

"You say your children are all doing well in school, they do not cause you any trouble and the two older ones have after-school jobs. What do you think they would say if you told them how you felt?"

I did not have an answer to his question but, with his words of encouragement, I decided that I would go home and share my thoughts with them.

That very evening while at the dinner table and before they left for work, I brought up the subject that I had been seeing a therapist, because I needed help sorting out some emotional problems. At first they looked at me with surprise. I was not supposed to need help with solving anything; I usually had been the one who solved the family problems. I explained to them that I had been feeling physically and emotionally exhausted and that I had been considering cutting back on my working hours to have a little more time for family duties and return to college for a few classes. They nodded but did not seem to understand the impact of what I was trying to say. I looked at each of their questioning faces and explained to them that my plan was difficult to put in motion because I could not possibly make ends meet if I worked less hours and received a smaller paycheck.

Both of my older children, who had part-time jobs, immediately offered to help out with household expenses. Mariane was only 12 and could not help financially, but her eyes told me that she too would have offered if she could. Relief must have been obvious on my face as I hugged each of them and my heart swelled with pride. For some reason fate had taken my husband, their father, away from us, but they more than made up for this loss. They were my salvation and my most precious assets. There and then, we all agreed that I would reduce my workload by at least a day or two a week.

The hospital personnel were agreeable except that it meant a change in my schedule. Instead of working on the same floor every day, I would now be assigned to all floors where help was needed, replacing nurses who called in sick, were on vacation or where the hospital floors were overloaded. I had been used to taking care of the same patients until they recovered and went home. I no longer got to know them or their parents because I now had different patients every day plus the increased demands of orienting myself to their needs, their medications and procedures. While this assignment turned out to be more demanding, I did acquire more time off for myself and used it wisely. I enrolled at Cypress Junior College to fulfill the necessary studies needed to later transfer to the California State University at Long Beach.

When I started attending college, I was so eager for learning that I wanted to just inhale the new experiences. I had not realized how out of touch I was with the changing times. I remember one day after class, I could not start my car. I saw a male student approaching his vehicle that was parked next to mine and asked him if he had jumper cables and would he help me start my car. He gladly obliged. After the car started and I was thanking him, he asked me if I had time to go for coffee.

"Thanks" I said, "but I have three kids waiting for me at home." He then asked me,

"Are you married?"

How stupid! I thought. You see in my day, first came love then came marriage and *then* came the baby carriage. It never even entered my mind that he could have thought I was divorced. I had been the ignorant one, or rather had not kept up with the evolving culture. This was the early 70's, the nation had dealt with flower-children, Woodstock, psychedelics and free love, while my experience was working hard, attending classes and supporting three children. So when he again asked me,

"Are you married?" I replied,

"I just told you I have three kids." He looked at me with surprise, or was it disbelief? Without another word he got in his car and drove away. I got in my car and drove home, to my yesteryears.

I graduated from Cypress College and started attending C.S.U.L.B. I had amazed myself at how well I was doing. My grades were close to 4.0 and I had even been invited to join the Phi Alpha Honorary Society. At this university I met Dr. Massaro. He taught a class in psychology that I was required to take for my major course of study in Social Welfare. In his class we hardly ever used the course textbooks. Instead, every morning, he would pick an item from the daily newspaper and somehow always managed to find a lesson in it.

Rather than have us read and simply memorize interpretations of authors, he prodded us to use our intuition and our own senses to ask and learn and find out things for ourselves. He forced us to think. Many college students signed up for his class and many had to wait another semester as it filled quickly. I had a great admiration for him. Still hurting from the loss of my husband, I hoped that he would teach me different coping methods, yet I was also still searching for sympathy.

One day after a class meeting, I lingered until everyone had left the room and then I approached him. After I told him how much I enjoyed his teaching technique and how I felt that it was helping me, I also related my problems and my fears about my husband's illness, his threats, his leaving us, my working and taking college classes, and raising three children alone. I was close to tears and very agitated when he interrupted me by saying,

"You are very lucky."

I looked at him incredulously, "Lucky?" He took my shaking hand in his,

"My dear," he said, "As you grow older you will learn that bad things happen to all of us sooner or later. No one goes through life untouched by sadness or misfortune. Some lose their possessions, some lose a child, a parent, or a mate and others suffer illnesses themselves. You have to bend with the storm and when it passes you must stand up straight again. It's all part of living."

"Why do you call that lucky?" I asked.

"Well you see," he went on, "as each of us face these tragedies in our own lives, many of us break. Some people commit suicide, or they may commit a crime and end up in jail. Others become invalids and some end up in a mental hospital. Depression is hard to overcome. You have been a survivor, so I consider you one of the lucky ones."

I stood there in silence. I started to grasp the meaning of his wise words. I remembered the time when I had considered suicide and how thoughts of my children and my responsibilities to them had dispelled that option. I reflected on my husband's incapacity and how he seemed determined not to get well. I took a deep breath. As Dr. Massaro let go of my hand, I noticed students rushing by in the hallway to catch their classes and wondered who amongst them would be a survivor and who would go under with the strain of whatever life had in store for them.

"Thank you" I mumbled as I shook his hand. He gave me a knowing smile and said nothing more as he picked up his notes in preparation for his next class. He had helped cast a light on the dark portion of my mind and made me realize that although I had no control over what happens, how I react to it was up to me. I now recall how Michael J. Fox, an actor who suffers from Parkinson's disease, named his autobiography "Lucky Man" and I am able to understand.

Going to classes on a part-time basis took me six years to complete my studies and, finally, in 1977 I graduated with a Bachelor of Arts Degree in Social Welfare. That major required numerous classes in Sociology and Psychology that were quite helpful on a personal level. I learned about different behaviors and cultures. I also studied the multitude of reasons why people behave in certain ways and the forces of upbringing that initiate responses. By the time I received my degree, I had also uncovered my own strengths and weaknesses. To me, graduation was much more than the parchment I received. It was a celebration of my spirit and newfound philosophy that if one puts their mind to something and stays with it, they will eventually succeed.

When overcome by stress I started reciting the Serenity Prayer,

> *God grant me the serenity*
> *To accept the things I cannot change;*
> *Courage to change the things I can;*
> *And wisdom to know the difference.*

It is never easy, but we are all where we are because of choices we have made, and doing nothing is also a choice. The crowning glory of my graduation came when my three children got together and invited all my friends for a graduation party. They were wonderful to plan this for me. The house was full of people I loved who had encouraged me throughout the years. The special event turned out to be a very joyous and memorable occasion for which I was truly grateful.

In the following years, I attended Jesse's graduation from C.S.U. in Fullerton, with a Bachelor of Science Degree in Biology and later a Master of Business Administration Degree from Pepperdine University. Dianne graduated with a Bachelor of Arts Degree in Graphic Design, also from C.S.U. in Fullerton, and did further studies at the Art Center of Design in Pasadena. Mariane earned her Associate of Arts Degree from Cypress College and also received certification in Pharmacy Technology.

It takes my breath away when I say all this because they have made me so proud and the credit is all theirs, having earned their tuition by working so very hard after school classes. They too had to make choices and they gave up most of their free time to achieve their goals.

Chapter Twenty-One

European Vacation

In the autumn of 1984, I dared myself to venture on my own on a five-week trip to Europe. I needed a vacation and also wanted to visit my family in Malta again. My parents had passed away, but I still had an aunt and uncle there as well as many cousins. I also felt a curious need to see how Tony was doing. I guess I was a glutton for punishment, but this tug in my heart for Tony never left me no matter how much I tried to overcome it. Because money was still tight, I opted to backpack and stay in hostels or other inexpensive rooms.

My plan was to start in England and take local southbound transportation to visit popular sights and eventually make my way to the island. I first stayed three days with a cousin in Surrey, about an hour's drive south of London. From there, I boarded a train to the port of Dover. Then I crossed the English Channel to Calais in France and took a second train to Paris, the 'City of Lights.' Here, I met my first challenge. It was dusk when I arrived at the busy train station filled with young backpackers. The areas surrounding the station usually offer abundant lodging at low rates. Unfortunately, everywhere I went the rooms had already been booked. One helpful landlady gave me some reliable advice,

"Arrive at a city in the morning and book your room for the night early." I would be sure to do that next time.

After walking with my backpack for almost three hours, darkness had settled in and I was so tired and felt so frustrated that I came close to wanting to return home. To my own amazement, I found that again when I felt up against a wall, I managed to find a way around it.

I entered another cheap looking hotel with crowds of young people huddled outside. As I expected, the hotel clerk told me that he had no more rooms to rent. I put down my backpack in the foyer and asked him to please help me find a place for the night, because I could not walk anymore and I may have to sleep on the floor. He picked up the phone and started making calls. I figured if he called the police, I would at least be taken to their station where there might be a cot to sleep on. Desperate moments demanded drastic measures.

To my delight he had not called the police but had found an available bed for me. He handed me a piece of paper directing me to the Metro, the underground rapid transit railway of Paris, which I had to take to reach the small hotel. I had never ridden the Metro before and by now it was after ten o'clock at night. One second I became very scared and a moment later I had nervous giggles... I could not believe I was doing this on my own.

I crossed the street and headed towards the entrance to the subway. A young man approached me and with limited English told me that he knew someone who rented out rooms. Relieved, I walked a while with him, but when he proceeded to leave the main road and approach a side street, a loud warning bell rang out in my head. He could have been honest, but I could not afford to take a chance on maybe getting mugged. I waved him *au revoir* and made my way back to the underground railway.

I found the Paris Metro something to behold. This subterranean transit station was brightly lit with stores all along the walkways leading to the platforms. It was like another city street beneath the avenues above, all alive with the hustle and bustle of people changing trains and others shopping at all hours amidst aspiring musicians soulfully playing a variety of instruments. I could easily forget that I was underground.

After I boarded, I approached a well-dressed couple and not being able to speak French, I pointed to my paper with the directions and to the 'X' marking my destination.

They showed me that all the terminals on each route were written in sequence at the top of every car and how at every station the location is posted in big letters on the platform. Checking my map, I could see that my last station was three stops away. Everything went smoothly and I managed to find my rooming house. Though the bed was soft and sagging, by then I could have slept on a rock.

The next morning, I was ready to tackle Paris. By midday, I had found my way to the Eiffel Tower, once the tallest structure in the world, and Notre Dame de Paris Cathedral, a Gothic masterpiece. I admired the tour boats traversing on the river Seine and had lunch at a street cafe on the prestigious Champs D'Elysee, while I enjoyed watching the people pass by. Riding the Metro had become a 'piece of cake.'

I went to the Louvre museum the following day. I wanted to see the most famous painting in the world, Leonardo da Vinci's *Mona Lisa,* along with other fantastic exhibits and works of art by renowned artists. A long line had already formed outside the museum by the time I arrived at 8 a.m. As always, I had my camera hanging around my neck, a fanny pack tied securely around my waist and my passport and credit card in a pouch inside my waistband. It looked like it was going to be a long wait.

A poorly dressed mother with three young sons in tow was walking up from the back of the line, her hands outstretched, begging for money. The sons appeared to be about ten or eleven years old and were also begging. As they approached, I began to feel very sorry for them. Here I was waiting to enter this fabulous museum while observing this pitiful scene. From my fanny pack, I pulled out a few French coins and placed them in the mother's hand. She nodded and moved to the person ahead of me. A couple of minutes later, I heard a commotion from about ten feet in front of me. The woman and the three children scattered, running in separate directions. This frail looking foursome could outrun a deer! I soon learned that the person in line ahead had been robbed of his camera and his wallet. The thieves were nowhere in sight. My travel guidebook had warned about such incidents, but one never expects them to happen right next to you and in broad daylight. I was glad that I had followed the instructions on how to carry my passport, credit card and camera, yet I was still dumbfounded to realize that while the four thieves were pretending to be begging, they were actually checking out each person to see who would be an easy prey.

The museum was as grandiose as it is acclaimed to be. I spent four hours there and could easily have spent four more. Later on, I regarded with wonder the French architecture, with its European flair, the elaborate water fountains and the magnificent, albeit expensive, Parisian shops.

With my self-confidence now back in gear, I traveled next to Barcelona, Spain, then to Nice in southern France, and on to Venice, Florence, and Rome in Italy. Each time I took the night train, arriving in the city by early morning. A benefit was that by paying a bit extra for a 'couchette' sleeping car, I saved a night's lodging. This four-bed cabin can be very crowded when full of occupants and all their luggage, but if it was a non-smoking car, I happily sometimes had the cabin all to myself.

When I was in Nice waiting for my train to take me to Venice, I sat at an outside table at a sidewalk café, and sipped on a small glass of wine. Music was blaring from a speaker above the doorway. I was contemplating how I had been in Barcelona, Spain, just two days earlier. Here I was in Nice, France, and tomorrow I would be in Venice, Italy. Three very different countries, each with their own language, culture and architecture, yet within such a short distance from each other. Suddenly, out of the speaker came the familiar voice of the then-current pop vocalist Cyndi Lauper singing, "Girls just wanna have fun."

How ironic, I thought, *an American song, to complete my international daydream.*

I laughed out loud, then became very self-conscious and looked around in embarrassment. Across from me at another table sat two American servicemen. Our eyes met and they gestured for me to join them. My feeling of bliss jumped another notch with this invitation… but maybe it was the wine. I waved, but declined joining them. Later in Venice, nothing pleased me as much as when one day a young backpacker said to me,

"It has been a pleasure meeting you, I wish my mother had the guts to do what you are doing."

Venice is the city of romance. Lovers on gondolas snuggling close together, while the gondoliers belt out melodic Italian arias as the boats glide through the winding canals and underneath the bridges. Cafes lined the large main square in front of St. Mark's Basilica and numerous doves fluttered around catching food tossed to them by tourists. It's a fairy-tale setting, with narrow canals everywhere you look.

This is the place where I felt most lonely. It brought memories of love lost and the pain of that loss seemed to pierce my heart. While crossing one of the bridges, I looked around and noticed people laughing everywhere. At the corner of one street, the sound of music drifted out from Harry's Bar, famous for having been Hemingway's watering hole. On the opposite corner, an old lady with a basket full of tidbits was busy feeding about fifteen cats. I marveled at the scenes passing in front of me and my heart again rejoiced. I tried hard to leave the past behind. This moment had to be treasured.

From Venice, I took the train to Rome. Rome is called the 'Eternal City' and rightfully deserves this name. Art is everywhere. St. Peter's Basilica, the Vatican Palace, the Sistine Chapel, the Boboli Gardens, the Trevi Fountain, La Scala Santa, the ancient Coliseum, and the Roman Forum make up a long list of 'must-see' places all in one enduring city. I toured the sites for two days and then took the train to Sicily where I boarded a ferry for the 60-mile crossing to Malta. This last stop, the highlight of my trip, would surely be a challenge to my emotions.

Chapter Twenty-Two

Highlight of My Trip

Malta is small, and while I cannot compare it to the beautiful places I had just witnessed, it has its own appeal and history. Sitting in the middle of the Mediterranean Sea, it is sometimes called 'Calypso Island,' as in Homer's *Odyssey* where Ulysses heard the sirens calling and had to be tied to the mast of his ship so he would not fall victim to their spell. My short trip was rough as the ship lurched through the unusually choppy sea. Nauseous, I reclined on a bench, deep in thought, recalling my childhood and did not even move when a ship's bell rang announcing an invitation to a small luncheon. Soon, the twinkling lights on the island glowed invitingly through the mist of the oncoming night. I anxiously looked forward to seeing family again.

I disembarked and easily passed through customs to find Aunt Evelyn and Uncle Joe waiting for me. Aunt Evelyn is my mother's youngest sister and the only one of her siblings still living. Their hospitality was greatly appreciated. She and my uncle have a beautiful villa at Kappara, a small town close to Sliema, the city where I was born. My uncle is an importer of Kraft food products from America and associates in Europe. He also owns a retail store on one of the main streets in Valetta, Malta's capital city, where his company sells packaged and frozen foods. My uncle also owns a manufacturing plant that produces a German detergent called Dixon.

They were thrilled to have me stay with them; in fact my aunt is of the old school and would have been offended had I stayed elsewhere. I soon learned that they had a daily maid, so my visit would not create any inconvenience or more work for my aunt. When I joined them for dinner, Aunt Evelyn proudly explained that she still did all the cooking. At this time, she had recently celebrated her 70th birthday and seemed to be in excellent health. She loved a good joke and had a good sense of humor, but as reigning matriarch of the family, she expected the respect due her position.

During my stay with them, I visited other relatives and also old friends and neighbors. Then I voiced my interest in seeing Tony. I knew that he still lived with his nephew John and his family a few miles away in the next town. My aunt expressed great concern, afraid of his reaction at seeing me again, but I had to see him. I wanted to find out how he was getting along, besides I knew that he would eventually find out that I was in Malta. Gossip travels fast on a small island where almost everyone knows everyone else, and I feared that neglecting to visit would have angered him. I called John the following morning and he invited me to join them for lunch the next day.

When we met, I could hardly believe the change. Tony's hair had turned gray and he was now slightly paunchy. He was only 56 years old, three years older than me, but his crooked smile and his half-closed right eye (residuals from the old surgery), made him look much older. I did not know how to greet him. I had not seen him for 14 years and most of our past turmoil was 'water under the bridge,' or so I hoped. I held out my hand and he embraced it in both of his. He seemed sincerely glad to see me; however, I could not guess what his thoughts were. Since I had divorced him so long ago, he had not made any effort to get in touch with me or our children, except for the initial old letters filled with anger and accusations.

John drove us to a nice little restaurant by the sea and we had a quiet lunch. We did not discuss the past or the future for which I was thankful. None of us seemed to want to risk saying anything that might upset the statue quo. On the way back to their home, as I sat in the back seat of the car next to Tony, he extended his hand and took hold of mine again. I did not want to pull it away and make him feel rejected. Neither did I want to hold his hand and imply that I wanted to reciprocate, so I let my hand stay limp in his. Unsure of Tony's intentions, as we entered the house, I whispered to his nephew and asked him not to leave us alone together.

We sat next to each other on the couch and John served us drinks, while his wife Theresa showed me family photos including their wedding pictures where Tony had been their Best Man. Soon however, she had to go upstairs to put the kids to bed. John went into the kitchen to get more ice cubes and Tony took this opportunity to move closer and attempt to kiss me and caress my breast. With his mouth close to my ear, he whispered,

"There is no divorce in Malta, you are still my wife."

I felt an overpowering fright and sprang up from the sofa. My sudden recoil at his touch was unexpected. It was as if I had been hit on the head with a hammer and all my cerebral nerves were jangled, yet fell back in the right places. It was as if my twin self was telling me,

"Alice wake up. You are not in wonderland any more."

Yes, I had wanted to see Tony again face-to-face, and this was it, the reality, not the expected fantasy I had built up.

For years I had filled my mind with fairytale endings. I wanted Tony back in our lives, but I also wished him to be well again. I wanted my family to be whole once more, but it was not meant to be. This sudden true and bare exposure to the truth proved very hard to handle. My head started throbbing, my stomach churned and I had to hold my hands together to stop them from shaking. My legs went weak. I knew that if I did not get out of the house, I might faint.

I finally had to face the fact of what was - the awakening of my reality – not of the far-fetched promise of togetherness, but of the finality of my dreams. It wasn't Tony's fault. He was just being himself, responding to feelings with no thought of yesterdays or tomorrows. I was the one who had held on to the impossible dream and now this sudden coming to my senses was very frightening.

"John" I yelled, "What is holding you up? Please hurry back."

Responding to my shrill voice, John immediately returned to the living room with the ice bucket. I am sure I appeared flustered. My face was burning and my hands had started to shake again. I did not understand my own mixed feelings; not wanting to hurt Tony but unable to return his passion. I experienced a sensation I had not been expecting, one of fear mixed with anger and sympathy. I had to get out of there. I mumbled something about the late hour and that my aunt would be worried as she had expected me to return home earlier. As I quickly headed towards the door, Tony grabbed my arm and said,

"We have to get together again before you leave."

"Yes." I promised, this time knowing full well that I was lying.

As John drove me back to my aunt's home, he expressed his regrets, but of course he wasn't to blame. I explained to him that I had no intention of seeing Tony again, because the situation was too charged given Tony's now obvious expectations and desires. I was feeling stressed and unable to cope. He seemed to understand.

When I told my aunt what had happened, she said that she knew that I should not have gone to see him. I wanted to agree with her, but had I not gone to see him, my guilt at rejecting him would have upset me just as much. At least this way I now knew that we could not have the friendship I had hoped for and I also realized, once and for all, that I could not ignore the past.

Looking back, I can see what a stupid mistake I had made. I had exposed myself to Tony's unpredictable behavior. Luckily at the time, he had not been hostile and just wanted to renew our relationship. But had he decided otherwise, it could just as easily have been a knife in my side. This episode had given me the final assurance that I needed to move on.

That night my head ached and I tossed in bed till morning. My aunt brought me tea and toast in bed and I stayed there all day. Just sitting up made me nauseous and the pain got so bad that I felt my head was about to split. My blood pressure must have soared to its very limits.

To stave off my migraine, for the next three days I plied myself with aspirins and stayed in my room trying to focus and collect my thoughts, while my dear aunt made me soups and sandwiches and tried her best to soothe me. By now, it was close to the end of my vacation. My plan had been to leave Malta via ship to Catania, Sicily, and then take the train back to Rome from where I planned to fly back home to Los Angeles. Feeling still unnerved and remembering how seasick I had become on the boat two weeks earlier, I changed my plans. I booked a plane to Rome instead with the intention of spending the last two days of my vacation there. My aunt understood my reasons for wanting to get away and was very supportive.

Since I had already toured Rome and I was only going to be there two days, I left my large backpack in a locker at the airport and with an overnight bag took a bus to the same hotel I had stayed in before. It was reasonably priced and familiar and when the hotel clerk saw me, he greeted,

"Oh, you are back. I have a better room for you this time."

It was a warm and welcome reception. I enjoyed being in Rome again. My spirits were restored and when I finally had to leave it was with regret. As my plane took off and I could see the large dome of the Vatican, the beautiful landscape of the Boboli Gardens and the shimmering blue Mediterranean Sea, my heart sang and my lips whispered the words to *Arrivederci Roma.* I had thrown a penny in the Trevi fountain and, as legend has it, those who do so will someday return!

Jesse and Mariane were waiting for me when I arrived at the Los Angeles airport. I had hoped that Dianne would also be there, but since she was absent I assumed she must have had to work. When we reached home, I was stunned to see why Dianne had not come to meet me. She had painted a huge ten-foot handmade banner with gigantic letters that read, "WELCOME HOME MOM!" Apparently, she had been busy mounting it across the whole front porch, when the others left to pick me up.

On our kitchen table was a large cake decorated with maps and the names of all the countries I had visited. It said, "Welcome Home Happy Wanderer."

Oh how wonderful it was to be home with my children again. What a blessing they were, and still are. That night I had a long and restful sleep.

Chapter Twenty-Three

Endings and Beginnings

We had no further communication with Tony and about five years later, in early January of 1989, we received a cable from his nephew informing us that Tony had been diagnosed with pancreatic cancer and did not have long to live. He had asked to see his children, so Jesse and Dianne decided to go and see him immediately. I am glad that they went because they were able to put aside years of resentment and make peace with their father. Although they will probably never forget, they made the effort to forgive. They told me he was happy to see them and that he had apparently accepted his impending death. They found him in a very feeble condition, with a great loss of weight and barely able to leave his hospital bed. I wish Mariane could have gone also, but unfortunately, at this time, she was in the midst of planning her approaching wedding and so chose not to accompany them. Jesse and Dianne returned home, mournful in the knowledge that their father was gravely ill and they would never see him again. They never showed me their last photos of their father, convincing me that it was better for me if I did not see his condition.

Mariane's wedding went on as planned. Jesse escorted her down the aisle and Dianne was her Maid of Honor. She was married on February 18, 1989.

When I saw Mariane walking towards the altar, so many thoughts crossed my mind. She looked so beautiful, so glorious, as she approached her husband-to-be, on her brother's arm. Her eyes shone and her whole being radiated happiness. Given that none of my children had had very happy adolescent years, I am so grateful that somehow they were able to overcome their misfortune. They are all now self-assured and able to sustain a positive outlook on life.

Tony passed away on March 5th 1989, just two weeks after Mariane's wedding. His death left me with very mixed feelings. I did not have to worry anymore that he could come back and hurt us. His niece had written and explained that he did not suffer for very long. He had lapsed into a coma and died soon after. I am glad about that. However, he had been in pain for many years both physically and emotionally. He had never been able to overcome his fears, his superstitions, or his erroneous belief that someone was out to harm him. I prayed that he was now at peace and I comforted myself with this. I had hung on to the belief that someday we might possibly be a family again. My hope for a long and happy married life—one that we all dream of on our wedding day—did not come about. I try not to question 'why' anymore because there is no answer. Yet how do you finalize something that you do not want to believe has really ended? How do you come to terms with the reality that you have denied to yourself for so very long? My dream of coming to America had come true and, somehow through all the family turmoil, our children had managed to excel. This chapter of my life had finally ended.

Things happen for a reason and we have to accept them and move on. I strongly believe in God's plan for us. I now also realize that had my husband not been sick and had our marriage not fallen apart, I would not have had reason to go to college for my nursing degree. We would probably also have disagreed on our children's upbringing and discipline. I can never know what the alternative outcome could have been, but I do know that when a door closes another one opens and, in retrospect, it's ultimately been to my benefit. Life experience has taught me that things do not often run smoothly. Change is evident all around us and we have to bend in the storm of our life, or we break.

As I now sit in my living room chair, I can see on the mantel the wedding pictures of my three children. How happy they look with their beaming smiles; the beautiful young brides dressed in flowing white dresses and the grooms in their formal attire. Who can tell what their future holds? That is why mothers cry at weddings. Not only from joy but from the knowledge that life is not always 'happily ever after.' I find comfort now in the knowledge that they have developed the strength and understanding to deal with life's ups and downs and I pray that their life experiences will help them grow, as I did.

I live alone, but I am not lonely. The children are grown and living their own lives and have given me the joys of many grandchildren and great-grandchildren. I have dear friends and siblings that I communicate with often. I actually have achieved something I never dreamed I would... I am now at peace.

While reality almost always does not live up to our fantasy, we have to continue believing in our dreams and when we encounter stumbling blocks we must kick them aside, climb over them, or change course and continue walking.

THE END